Expense Stability

How to Control Spending, Reduce Leakage, and Create Consistency

Mark Ellison

PERENNIAL PUBLISHING

Published by Perennial Publishing

First Edition

Paperback ISBN: 978-971996-18-9
Hardcover ISBN: 978-971996-19-6
EBook ISBN: 978-971996-20-2

For bulk or institutional orders, contact Perennial Publishing.

Contents

Introduction

Expenses are commonly treated as the most visible part of personal finance and the least structurally understood. They are usually described as choices, habits, preferences, or failures of restraint. In that framing, instability appears to begin with behavior, and correction appears to depend on better decisions. The result is a narrow way of thinking about outflow: expenses are reduced to acts of spending rather than recognized as demands placed on a system. That distinction matters because systems do not become unstable merely because decisions occur. They become unstable because load behaves in ways the structure cannot absorb.

This book begins from a different premise. Expenses are not first a behavioral category. They are not best understood as expressions of impulse, discipline, or lifestyle drift. They are a form of load applied to a financial system over time. Once they are seen that way, the central question changes. The issue is no longer whether spending appears reasonable in isolation. The issue is whether outflow (load, as structured demand) remains absorbable by the available capacity (income and liquidity) that supports it. This reframing moves expenses out of the language of correction and into the language of system behavior.

That shift is necessary because the ordinary treatment of financial stability places too much explanatory weight on income. A household is often assumed to be stable if inflow is large enough, rising quickly enough, or generally viewed as sufficient. But income by itself does not determine whether a system remains stable under ordinary operation or disruption. High income can coexist with recurring pressure, rapid depletion of liquidity, short runway, and fragile dependence on timing precision. The appearance of capacity is not the same as structural stability. What matters is the relationship between load and capacity, not the size of inflow viewed alone.

This is why instability persists in systems that appear strong when measured only by earnings. If expenses are rigid, poorly timed, highly variable, concentrated, or misaligned with the structure of inflow, then capacity is continually forced into compensation. Liquidity becomes a bridge rather than a buffer for absorbing load. Runway shortens faster than expected. Pressure appears even when totals seem sufficient. The system does not fail because income is absent in absolute terms. It becomes unstable because outflow behaves in ways that continually test or exceed what the structure can support at the intervals that matter. In that sense, expenses are not secondary to stability. They are one of its primary determinants.

The central problem, then, is not spending in the abstract. It is outflow structure. Expenses matter because of how they behave over time. Timing creates sequencing gaps when demand arrives before support. Distribution concentrates load, creating pressure even when totals are unchanged. Persistence defines the system's floor and limits flexibility. Variability introduces instability through irregular movement, and rigidity prevents adjustment when conditions change. What appears to be ordinary expense activity is often the mechanical source of instability once these structural features are made visible.

This book is built around that visibility. It treats expenses not as entries in a spending record but as active forces applied to a system over time. Seen this way, outflow does not merely reduce balance. It shapes pressure formation, determines liquidity use, compresses runway, amplifies stress, and defines whether disruption remains absorbable. The question is not whether expenses exist. Every functioning system operates under load. The question is whether that load is structured in a way that allows continuity.

Stability, in this framework, is not the result of generic restraint and not the reward for simply spending less. It refers to a system condition in which load remains continuously absorbable over time without repeatedly forcing the system into pressure, disorder, or reserve-dependent compensation. That condition depends on structure: on the relationship between baseline demand and capacity, on the distribution of outflow over time, on the distance between load and failure thresholds, on the interaction between expenses and liquidity, and on the degree to which outflow remains controlled, aligned, and adaptable. Stability is therefore not a mood, a strategy, or a temporary state of caution. It reflects the behavior of a system whose demands remain structurally supportable.

That point is easy to miss when expense analysis is reduced to reduction. If expenses are viewed only through the lens of lowering totals, then the deeper mechanics of instability remain hidden. A system can lower some expenses and remain fragile if the remaining load is badly timed, highly rigid, or poorly aligned with inflow. It can carry relatively high expenses and remain stable if those expenses are bounded, distributed, synchronized, and supportable relative to capacity. This is why amount alone does not explain system behavior. A stable expense system is not defined by smallness. It is defined by absorbability.

That is also why this book does not proceed as a budgeting manual, a discipline argument, or a series of corrective prescriptions. It does not ask how expenses should be judged morally, and it does not treat financial control as a matter of personal restraint. Those approaches misidentify the level at which the problem exists. This book operates at the level of structure. It models how expense systems behave under load, how they respond to variability and disruption, how they absorb or fail to absorb pressure, and how their design determines whether continuity can be maintained over time. The emphasis is not on advice but on mechanism.

That difference in method matters because mechanism changes what becomes visible. Once expenses are treated as system load, familiar categories begin to behave differently. Fixed expenses become baseline demand rather than merely recurring bills. Variable expenses become moving load rather than incidental fluctuation. Discretionary expenses become adjustable layers of demand rather than moral categories of restraint. Liquidity becomes short-term absorptive capacity rather than a vague form of prudence. Runway becomes time-to-failure rather than a general sense of safety. Alignment becomes the coordination of inflow and outflow rather than a loose idea of balance. Flexibility becomes system adaptability rather than willingness to change. In each case, the system view replaces the behavioral view by shifting attention from judgment to structure.

The chapters that follow build this view in sequence. They move from formal definition into composition, baseline, variability, pressure, stress, drift, timing, shock, feedback, control, reduction, smoothing, constraint, margin, liquidity, runway, interaction, alignment, flexibility, and resilience. But the purpose of that progression is not to accumulate terminology for its own sake. It is to show that expense stability is a coherent operating model. Each mechanism adds a layer to the same system: how outflow behaves, how support absorbs it, how instability forms, and how continuity is either preserved or broken.

For that reason, this book is best read as a structural argument rather than as a collection of isolated insights. The concepts are cumulative because the system is cumulative. Baseline shapes margin. Variability affects pressure. Pressure becomes stress when unresolved. Stress consumes liquidity and shortens runway. Timing affects how much liquidity must bridge. Alignment reduces avoidable friction. Flexibility changes how the system responds under disruption. Constraint limits what load can become before it enters the system. These are not separate topics in the ordinary sense. They are interlocking parts of one operating structure. To understand any one of them fully requires understanding the others as connected mechanisms.

The reader should therefore approach this book in the same spirit in which one would approach any system analysis: not by looking for immediate prescriptions, but by learning how the structure behaves. The purpose is not to deliver tactics detached from context. It is to clarify what expenses are doing inside the system, what kinds of load create fragility, what kinds of structure preserve absorbability, and why stability depends on continuity of controlled outflow rather than on simple reduction or temporary caution. This shift in perspective is the real beginning of the book.

Once that shift is made, the logic of expense stability becomes clearer. Expenses are not best understood as behaviors to be judged. They are better understood as loads to be modeled. Stability is not best understood as spending less. It is better understood as structural alignment between demand and the capacity available to absorb it. The work of this book is to define that alignment, trace the mechanisms that preserve or break it, and establish a rigorous language for how expense systems remain stable or become unstable over time.

The next step is to define that system formally. Chapter 1 begins there, with the core condition on which the rest of the book depends: expense stability itself.

Expense Stability

Expense stability is not a function of how much is spent, but of how the system absorbs what is spent over time. It is defined structurally as the condition in which expense load remains consistently within the system's capacity, allowing continuity without pressure accumulation. This definition immediately separates stability from magnitude and anchors it in the interaction between load and capacity. The system does not evaluate whether expenses are "high" or "low," only whether they are sustainable relative to available capacity.

This leads to a critical distinction: stability is not a static state but a dynamic condition maintained over time. Expense load is continuously applied, and capacity is continuously responding. Stability exists only when this interaction remains aligned under changing conditions. When load remains within capacity, pressure does not accumulate, and the system maintains operational continuity.

This condition defines expense stability as a structural relationship rather than a behavioral outcome. The system does not rely on intent or adjustment; it reflects the configuration of load relative to capacity. If that configuration allows sustained absorption, stability is present. If not, pressure forms, and instability begins to develop.

Expense stability, therefore, is the baseline condition of a functioning financial system. It establishes whether the system can operate without entering stress states. Every subsequent concept builds on this definition, reinforcing that stability is determined by load versus capacity, not by spending level.

Expenses function as load applied to the system. Each expense introduces force that must be absorbed by available capacity. This load is defined not only by amount, but also by timing, frequency, and structure. A single expense may be small in magnitude but disruptive in timing, increasing pressure if it aligns poorly with capacity availability.

This means expense load is not uniform. It is distributed over time in patterns that determine how pressure forms within the system. Regular, predictable expenses create a consistent load profile, while irregular or clustered expenses create spikes. These spikes increase localized pressure, even if total load remains unchanged.

This relationship shows how expense stability is influenced by structure rather than totals. Two systems with identical expense totals can exhibit different stability outcomes depending on how load is distributed. Concentrated load increases pressure intensity, while distributed load allows smoother absorption within capacity.

As load accumulates, the system must continuously absorb it without exceeding capacity. If load exceeds available capacity at any point in time, pressure begins to form. This pressure is not abstract; it is the direct result of load interacting with insufficient capacity. Expense stability depends on maintaining load within the system's absorptive range across all time intervals.

Capacity functions as the counterforce to expense load, composed of income (inflow) and liquidity (buffer). It represents the system's ability to absorb load without generating pressure. Capacity consists of income flow and available liquidity, both of which determine how much load can be sustained at any given moment. Unlike load, which is applied externally through expenses, capacity is the internal response mechanism.

This leads to an important structural condition: capacity is not static. It fluctuates based on income timing, liquidity availability, and system configuration. A system with high total capacity may still experience pressure if that capacity is not accessible when load is applied. Timing misalignment between load and capacity creates localized instability.

This condition defines capacity as both magnitude and availability. It is not sufficient for capacity to exist; it must be accessible at the moment load is applied. When capacity is delayed or fragmented, the system experiences pressure even if total capacity exceeds total load.

This relationship determines expense stability by defining the system's ability to counteract load continuously. When capacity consistently matches or exceeds load at all points in time, stability is maintained. When capacity fails to meet load at any point, pressure forms, initiating instability. Capacity, therefore, is not simply a resource; it is the active counterforce that determines whether load generates pressure.

Stability emerges when load and capacity are aligned over time. This alignment means that at every point where load is applied, sufficient capacity is available to absorb it without generating pressure. The system operates smoothly because load is continuously matched by counterforce, preventing the accumulation of stress.

This leads to a structural definition of alignment. It is not enough for total capacity to equal total load; alignment requires synchronization. Load must be met by capacity at the exact moments it occurs. Misalignment in timing introduces pressure, even when totals suggest balance.

This condition defines stability as a continuous equilibrium rather than a periodic balance. The system does not reset at intervals; it operates continuously. Each moment of load application requires corresponding capacity. If alignment is maintained, pressure remains minimal, and stability persists.

This relationship shows that expense stability is a function of synchronization. When load and capacity are aligned, the system absorbs expenses without disruption. When alignment fails, pressure begins to form, even if only temporarily. Sustained alignment prevents pressure accumulation, preserving stability over time.

Instability arises when load and capacity become misaligned. This misalignment occurs when expense load exceeds available capacity at any point in time, creating pressure within the system. Pressure is the immediate signal of instability, indicating that the system cannot fully absorb the applied load.

This leads to the progression from pressure to stress. When misalignment is temporary, pressure may dissipate as capacity catches up. However, repeated or sustained misalignment causes pressure to accumulate, transitioning into stress. Stress reflects a system operating beyond its stable configuration, where recovery becomes increasingly difficult.

This condition defines instability not as failure, but as a process. It begins with pressure formation and escalates through continued misalignment. Each instance of load exceeding capacity contributes to this process, compounding the system's inability to maintain stability.

This relationship shows that instability is structural, not situational. It is not caused by a single expense but by the repeated interaction of load and insufficient capacity. Expense stability fails when misalignment becomes persistent, allowing pressure to evolve into sustained stress within the system.

Expense stability is often confused with low spending, but the two are structurally unrelated. Low spending reduces load magnitude, but it does not guarantee alignment with capacity. A system with low expenses can still experience instability if those expenses are poorly timed or concentrated.

This leads to a critical distinction: stability depends on the relationship between load and capacity, not on minimizing load. Reducing expenses may lower pressure, but it does not address misalignment. A system can maintain high expense levels and remain stable if capacity is sufficient and synchronized.

This condition defines stability as a configuration problem rather than a reduction problem. Lowering load without addressing structure may temporarily reduce pressure, but it does not ensure sustained stability. Conversely, maintaining higher load within aligned capacity preserves stability without requiring reduction.

This relationship shows that expense stability cannot be evaluated through spending levels alone. Stability emerges from how load interacts with capacity. Low spending may reduce pressure, but only alignment prevents instability. The system evaluates structure, not magnitude.

Consistency and predictability shape how load interacts with capacity over time. When expense load is consistent, the system can anticipate and match capacity accordingly. Predictable load reduces variability, allowing capacity to be structured in alignment with expected demand.

This leads to a reduction in pressure formation. When load is predictable, capacity can be positioned to absorb it without disruption. Irregular or unpredictable expenses introduce variability, increasing the likelihood of misalignment and pressure spikes. Variability, therefore, becomes a key driver of instability through increased misalignment risk.

This condition defines consistency as a stabilizing force within the system. It does not reduce load but organizes it in a way that aligns with capacity. Predictability allows the system to maintain equilibrium, preventing sudden increases in pressure.

This relationship shows that expense stability improves when load patterns are consistent and predictable. The system can sustain alignment more effectively, reducing the frequency and intensity of pressure events. Stability is therefore reinforced through predictable load behavior.

Control refers to the system's ability to adjust load in response to capacity conditions. Constraint, by contrast, represents boundary-enforced or inflexible expenses that must be absorbed regardless of capacity.

This leads to a structural distinction between flexible and rigid load. Flexible load allows the system to manage pressure by adjusting demand. Rigid load increases pressure because it cannot be modified in response to capacity limitations. The presence of rigid load reduces the system's ability to maintain stability.

This condition defines control as a key factor in expense stability. Systems with higher control can adapt to fluctuations in capacity, preventing misalignment. Systems with high constraint are more susceptible to pressure formation because load cannot be adjusted.

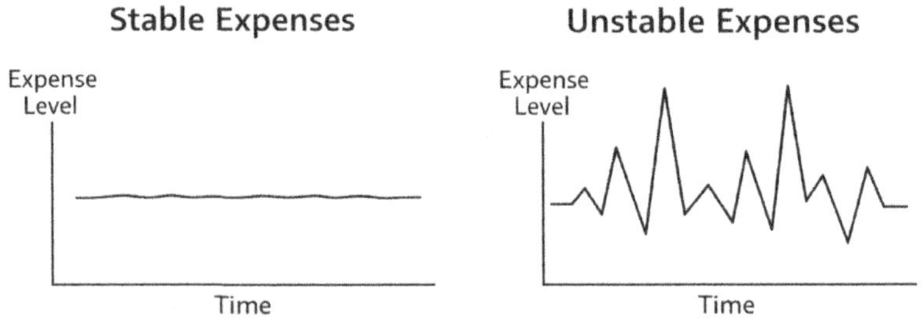

[Figure 1: Stable vs Unstable Expense Patterns — smooth consistent outflow vs irregular spikes]

This relationship shows that stability is influenced not only by load magnitude but by load flexibility. Controllable expenses allow the system to maintain alignment, while constrained expenses increase the risk of instability. Expense stability depends on the system's ability to manage load relative to capacity.

Instability originates from structural conditions that disrupt load-capacity alignment. These sources include variability in expense timing, concentration of load, and insufficient or poorly timed capacity. Each of these factors contributes to pressure formation within the system.

This leads to the identification of instability as a product of interaction rather than isolated events. A single expense does not create instability unless it interacts with insufficient capacity. The system becomes unstable when multiple factors combine to produce sustained misalignment.

This condition defines sources of instability as structural weaknesses. These weaknesses increase the likelihood that load will exceed capacity, generating pressure. Over time, repeated exposure to these conditions compounds instability, making recovery more difficult.

This relationship shows that expense stability requires identifying and understanding these sources. Stability is preserved when structural weaknesses are minimized, allowing load and capacity to remain aligned. Instability emerges when these weaknesses persist, increasing pressure within the system.

The expense system operates continuously, not in discrete intervals. Load is applied at specific moments, but the system's response is ongoing. Capacity must be available at all times to absorb load, making stability a continuous condition rather than a periodic outcome.

This leads to the concept of continuous pressure monitoring. The system does not evaluate stability monthly or annually; it reflects the immediate interaction of load and capacity. Each moment of misalignment contributes to pressure, regardless of overall totals.

This condition defines expense stability as a real-time property. The system must maintain alignment at all times to prevent pressure accumulation. Temporary misalignment may not result in immediate failure, but repeated instances contribute to instability.

This relationship shows that stability cannot be assessed through aggregate measures alone. Continuous system behavior requires evaluating how load and capacity interact over time. Stability exists when alignment is maintained consistently, not just on average.

Expense stability is a property of the system itself, not an outcome of individual decisions. It emerges from the configuration of load and capacity, independent of intent or effort. The system behaves according to its structure, producing stability or instability based on that configuration.

This leads to a shift in evaluation. Stability is not achieved through actions but through system design. The arrangement of load and capacity determines whether pressure forms. The system reflects its structure continuously, regardless of external perception.

This condition defines stability as inherent to the system. It cannot be imposed temporarily or achieved through isolated changes. Stability exists only when the system's configuration supports continuous alignment between load and capacity.

This relationship shows that expense stability must be understood as a structural property. It is not reactive or situational; it is embedded in how the system operates. Pressure, therefore, is not an anomaly but a signal of structural misalignment.

Expense stability forms the foundation of the entire financial system. It determines whether the system can operate without entering pressure and stress states. Without stability, all other components are compromised, as load continuously exceeds capacity.

This leads to the recognition that stability precedes optimization. Before growth, accumulation, or expansion can occur, the system must maintain alignment between load and capacity. Without this foundation, instability propagates through all subsequent layers.

This condition defines expense stability as the baseline requirement for system functionality. It ensures that load is absorbed without generating pressure, allowing continuity over time. Without it, the system remains in a state of persistent stress.

This relationship shows that expense stability is not one component among many; it is the primary condition that enables all others. By maintaining alignment between load and capacity, the system preserves stability, preventing pressure from escalating into breakdown.

Expenses as System Load

Expenses operate as active load applied to the system, not passive outputs or residual spending. Each expense introduces force that must be absorbed by capacity, creating immediate interaction between outflow (load) and the system's absorptive structure. This reframing establishes that expenses are not descriptive artifacts of behavior but active drivers of system conditions. Load is applied whether the system is prepared or not, and its effects are determined by how it interacts with capacity.

This mechanism defines load as continuous and force-generating. Every expense event introduces the potential for pressure, which becomes actual pressure when capacity is insufficient at that moment. The system does not interpret intent; it responds mechanically to load application. This establishes expenses as the initiating force behind all pressure formation within the system.

Over time, active load creates a persistent demand environment. Each expense adds to the system's required absorption, and the sequence of these applications determines whether pressure remains contained or begins to accumulate. Stable systems maintain alignment between load and capacity at each application point, preventing pressure escalation.

By contrast, unstable systems experience repeated instances in which load exceeds available capacity. This transforms expenses from neutral transactions into sources of stress. The defining condition is not the presence of expenses, but the force they apply relative to capacity, making load the primary determinant of system behavior.

Load is applied sequentially over time rather than in aggregate totals. Each expense occurs at a specific moment, requiring immediate capacity to absorb it. This temporal application means the system experiences load as a series of discrete forces, not as a summed figure. The sequence and spacing of these forces determine how pressure forms.

This mechanism defines timing as central to load behavior. When expenses are distributed evenly, capacity can respond in a stable pattern, maintaining alignment. When expenses cluster, multiple load events occur within narrow intervals, increasing the likelihood that capacity will be insufficient at those points.

Over time, sequential load application creates cumulative interaction effects. Even if total load remains constant, variations in timing alter how pressure develops. Stable systems distribute load in a way that aligns with capacity availability, reducing pressure spikes. Unstable systems concentrate load, creating intervals in which outflow exceeds inflow.

The contrast is structural rather than numerical. Identical totals produce different outcomes depending on sequencing. Stability depends on whether each load event can be absorbed as it occurs, reinforcing that time-based application governs pressure formation.

Inflow and outflow interact as opposing forces within the system. Inflow represents incoming capacity through income, liquidity provides stored capacity available for absorption, and outflow represents load applied through expenses. Stability depends on how these forces align at each point in time, not on their cumulative totals.

This mechanism defines interaction as dynamic and continuous. Inflow does not automatically offset outflow; it must be available when load is applied. Misalignment between inflow timing and outflow timing creates intervals in which load exceeds capacity, generating pressure. The system operates through this ongoing interaction, not through periodic reconciliation.

Over time, the balance between inflow and outflow determines whether pressure remains contained or begins to accumulate. Stable systems maintain synchronization, ensuring that inflow supports outflow as it occurs. Unstable systems experience gaps in which outflow persists without corresponding inflow.

The contrast highlights that income alone does not ensure stability. A system may have sufficient inflow in total but still experience pressure due to timing mismatches. Stability emerges from synchronized interaction, not from aggregate equality.

Pressure forms when load exceeds available inflow at any interval. This condition represents the moment when load surpasses capacity, creating immediate pressure within the system. Pressure is not gradual in origin; it begins at the exact point of imbalance between load and capacity.

This mechanism defines pressure as a direct output of structural misalignment. When expenses are applied without sufficient inflow support, the system must compensate through liquidity or deferment, both of which indicate pressure presence. The system does not absorb excess load without consequence; it converts it into pressure.

Over time, repeated instances of outflow exceeding inflow create a pattern of pressure formation. Each occurrence contributes to the system's overall stress, increasing the likelihood of stress accumulation. Stable systems minimize these occurrences by maintaining alignment, while unstable systems experience them frequently.

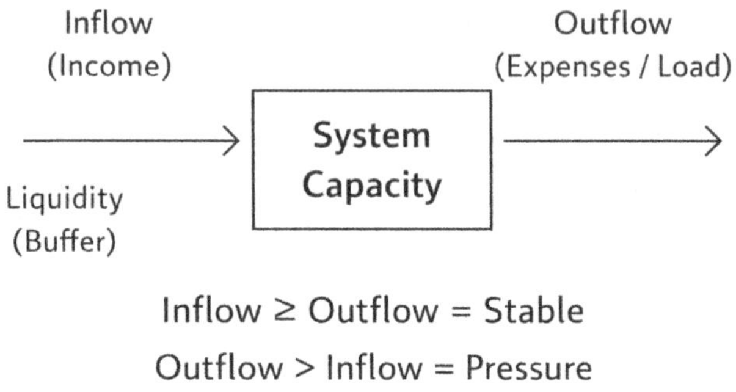

[Figure 2: Expenses as Load — inflow vs outflow pressure relationship]

The contrast is immediate and structural. When inflow meets outflow, no pressure forms, and the system remains stable. When outflow exceeds inflow, pressure is generated instantly. This binary condition defines the threshold between stability and instability.

Load persists when expenses recur across intervals, creating continuous demand on the system. Unlike one-time expenses, persistent load establishes an ongoing requirement for capacity absorption. This transforms the system from handling isolated events to managing sustained force application.

This mechanism defines persistence as a structural property of recurring expenses. Fixed obligations and repeated expenditures maintain constant load presence, reducing the system's ability to recover between intervals. Persistent load ensures that capacity must remain continuously available.

Over time, persistent load limits the system's flexibility. Each interval begins with pre-existing demand, leaving less capacity available for additional load. Stable systems maintain alignment despite this persistence, ensuring that recurring load remains within capacity. Unstable systems experience compounding pressure as persistent load interacts with fluctuating inflow.

The contrast shows that temporary load can be absorbed and dissipated, while persistent load requires continuous capacity alignment. Expense stability depends on whether persistent load remains sustainable relative to inflow, reinforcing its role in pressure formation.

Load accumulates when outflow exceeds inflow and the unmet portion carries forward into subsequent intervals. This accumulation represents unabsorbed demand that adds to future load, increasing total system pressure. The system does not reset between intervals; it retains the effects of prior imbalance.

This mechanism defines accumulation as a compounding process. Each instance of excess load contributes to a growing backlog that must be addressed by future capacity. Accumulated load increases the system's baseline pressure, making subsequent alignment more difficult.

Over time, accumulation transforms isolated pressure events into sustained stress. Stable systems prevent accumulation by ensuring that each interval's load is fully absorbed. Unstable systems allow load to carry forward, creating a cycle in which pressure compounds into stress.

The contrast illustrates that accumulation is the transition from temporary imbalance to structural instability. When load is contained within each interval, pressure dissipates. When load accumulates, pressure persists and intensifies, defining the pathway to system stress.

Load magnitude alone does not determine system stability; distribution over time governs how that load interacts with capacity. A large but evenly distributed load may be absorbed without pressure, while a smaller but concentrated load can exceed capacity and create instability.

This mechanism defines distribution as a structural determinant of pressure formation. Even distribution allows capacity to respond consistently, maintaining alignment. Concentrated distribution creates spikes in which load exceeds available capacity, generating pressure despite lower totals.

Over time, distribution shapes the system's exposure to pressure. Stable systems maintain smooth load patterns that align with inflow, reducing variability. Unstable systems experience irregular load distribution, increasing the frequency and intensity of pressure events.

The contrast emphasizes that totals are insufficient for evaluating stability. Identical magnitudes produce different outcomes based on distribution. Expense stability depends on how load is structured over time, not simply how much load exists.

High income does not eliminate instability when load remains high relative to capacity. A system with substantial inflow can still experience pressure if outflow is structured in a way that exceeds available capacity at critical intervals. Income increases capacity, but it does not control load.

This mechanism defines the separation between inflow magnitude and load structure. High-income systems often sustain higher levels of load, increasing their exposure to pressure formation. When load expands to match or exceed capacity, stability is not improved.

Over time, systems with high income but poorly structured load experience the same pressure dynamics as lower-income systems. Stability depends on alignment, not on absolute inflow levels. When load grows faster than effective capacity, pressure persists regardless of income.

The contrast shows that income is not the driver of stability. Systems with lower income but aligned load can remain stable, while high-income systems with excessive load experience instability. Load structure determines outcomes, reinforcing its role as the primary system force.

System stress emerges directly from load exceeding capacity over time. When pressure persists across intervals, it transitions into stress, representing accumulated stress within the system. This stress results from repeated imbalance between load and capacity.

This mechanism defines stress as the outcome of unresolved pressure. Each instance of excess load contributes to the system's overall stress level. As stress increases, the system's ability to absorb future load diminishes, creating a feedback loop that amplifies instability.

Over time, load-induced stress reduces system resilience. Stable systems prevent stress by maintaining alignment and dissipating pressure quickly. Unstable systems allow pressure to persist, leading to sustained stress and reduced capacity effectiveness.

The contrast highlights that stress is not caused by isolated events but by continuous load imbalance. When load remains within capacity, pressure does not accumulate, and stress is avoided. When load repeatedly exceeds capacity, stress becomes an inherent system condition.

The system operates under continuous load conditions, where expenses are always present and interacting with capacity. There is no state in which load is absent; the system constantly processes outflow against available inflow. This continuous environment defines how stability must be maintained.

This mechanism defines continuity as a fundamental property of the system. Load is not episodic but ongoing, requiring capacity to respond at all times. The system cannot rely on periodic adjustments; it must sustain alignment continuously to prevent pressure.

Over time, continuous load creates a baseline level of demand that shapes system behavior. Stable systems maintain capacity that matches this ongoing demand, preventing pressure accumulation. Unstable systems experience persistent misalignment, leading to recurring pressure.

The contrast demonstrates that stability cannot be achieved through intermittent balance. Continuous load requires continuous alignment. Expense stability depends on the system's ability to operate under constant load without generating pressure.

Load functions as the primary driver of system behavior because it initiates all interactions within the system. Capacity reacts to load, and pressure emerges from load exceeding capacity. Without load, there is no demand on the system, and no pressure formation occurs.

This mechanism defines load as the origin of system dynamics. While capacity determines how load is absorbed, it does not create demand. Load sets the conditions under which the system operates, making it the central force shaping outcomes.

Over time, variations in load determine how the system evolves. Stable systems manage load in alignment with capacity, maintaining equilibrium. Unstable systems experience excessive or poorly structured load, leading to pressure and stress.

The contrast clarifies that income and capacity are reactive elements, while load is proactive. Stability is not achieved by increasing capacity alone; it requires managing the force that drives system interaction. Load defines the system's trajectory.

Expenses function as a structural force that determines system stability through their role as load. They are not incidental components but the dominant mechanism through which pressure is generated or avoided. The structure of expenses defines how load interacts with capacity over time.

This mechanism positions expenses as the central determinant of system conditions. By shaping load magnitude, timing, and distribution, expenses control how pressure forms and whether it accumulates into stress. The system reflects the structure of its expenses continuously.

Over time, this structural force governs whether stability is maintained. Stable systems configure expenses in alignment with capacity, preventing pressure accumulation. Unstable systems allow expense structure to exceed capacity, generating persistent stress.

The contrast reinforces that expenses are not passive outcomes but active forces shaping system behavior. Expense stability depends on how this force is structured relative to capacity. As a result, expenses define the boundary between stability and instability within the system.

Fixed vs. Variable vs. Discretionary Expenses

Expenses must be classified by structural behavior rather than by descriptive type because stability is determined by how load interacts with capacity over time. This classification separates expenses into categories based on persistence, variability, and adjustability, which directly influence pressure formation. The system does not evaluate expenses by purpose but by how they behave under capacity constraint. This establishes classification as a functional requirement for understanding load dynamics.

This mechanism defines structural classification as the mapping of expense behavior to system impact. Fixed, variable, and discretionary categories represent distinct forms of load, each interacting with capacity in different ways. These distinctions determine how pressure emerges, dissipates, or accumulates across intervals. Without classification, load appears homogeneous, obscuring the mechanisms that drive instability.

Over time, structural classification allows the system to anticipate how different types of load will behave under changing capacity conditions. Fixed expenses maintain consistent demand, variable expenses introduce fluctuation, and discretionary expenses provide adjustment potential. Stable systems recognize and align these behaviors with capacity, preventing pressure accumulation.

The contrast is clear: systems that treat expenses as uniform cannot identify sources of pressure, while systems that classify them structurally can manage alignment. Expense stability depends on understanding how each category contributes to load-capacity interaction, making classification foundational to system behavior.

Fixed expenses function as baseline load that defines the minimum continuous demand on the system. These expenses persist across intervals and require capacity to absorb them regardless of changing conditions. This establishes a structural floor of load that must be supported at all times.

This mechanism defines baseline load as non-optional demand. Fixed expenses are applied continuously, creating a constant interaction with capacity. Because they do not adjust in response to capacity fluctuations, they represent the system's minimum required absorption level. This baseline determines the threshold below which capacity cannot fall without generating pressure.

Over time, baseline load reduces the system's available capacity for absorbing additional load. Each interval begins with fixed demand already applied, limiting flexibility. Stable systems maintain baseline load within reliable capacity, ensuring that this persistent demand does not generate pressure. Unstable systems set baseline load above sustainable capacity, creating continuous pressure.

The contrast shows that baseline load can either anchor stability or drive instability. When fixed expenses align with capacity, they create predictable load that can be absorbed consistently. When they exceed capacity, pressure becomes constant, defining instability at the system's core.

Fixed expense rigidity describes the inability of baseline load to adjust in response to capacity changes. This rigidity limits the system's flexibility, increasing the likelihood that load will exceed capacity under constrained conditions. Fixed expenses continue to apply load regardless of inflow variation.

This mechanism defines rigidity as structural inflexibility. When capacity decreases or becomes misaligned, rigid load cannot be reduced or delayed. This creates immediate pressure because the system must absorb fixed demand without adjustment. Rigidity transforms baseline load into a potential source of instability.

Over time, rigid load amplifies pressure during periods of reduced capacity. Each interval maintains the same fixed demand, even as inflow fluctuates. Stable systems maintain fixed load at levels that remain absorbable under varying capacity conditions. Unstable systems carry rigid load that exceeds capacity during disruptions, causing repeated pressure formation.

The contrast highlights that flexibility determines how systems respond to constraint. Systems with lower rigidity can adjust load to maintain alignment, while highly rigid systems cannot. Fixed expense rigidity therefore directly reduces the system's ability to preserve stability under changing conditions.

Variable expenses function as fluctuating load, changing in magnitude across intervals. Unlike fixed expenses, they do not maintain a constant level of demand, introducing variability into the system. This variability alters how load interacts with capacity over time.

This mechanism defines fluctuating load as magnitude variability. Variable expenses increase or decrease based on conditions, creating uneven load application. These changes can align with capacity or diverge from it, depending on timing and distribution. Variability introduces uncertainty into the system's load profile, increasing misalignment risk.

Over time, fluctuating load creates intervals of both lower and higher demand. Stable systems maintain variable load within ranges that capacity can absorb, preventing pressure spikes. Unstable systems experience large fluctuations that exceed capacity at certain points, generating pressure even if average load remains manageable.

The contrast demonstrates that variability is not inherently destabilizing but becomes so when it exceeds capacity thresholds. Systems with controlled variability maintain alignment, while systems with uncontrolled fluctuations experience repeated pressure formation. Variable expenses therefore act as a dynamic modifier of load behavior.

Variability introduces instability when fluctuations in load create unpredictable pressure events. This occurs when variable expenses exceed capacity during certain intervals, even if they remain within capacity on average. Variability increases the difficulty of maintaining consistent alignment.

This mechanism defines variability as a source of unpredictability in load application. When load magnitude changes irregularly, capacity may not be positioned to absorb it at each interval. This misalignment produces intermittent pressure, which can accumulate if not resolved.

Over time, repeated variability-driven pressure events contribute to system stress. Each spike that exceeds capacity generates pressure, and frequent spikes prevent the system from stabilizing. Stable systems manage variability within predictable bounds, ensuring that fluctuations do not exceed capacity. Unstable systems experience irregular and excessive variability, increasing pressure frequency.

The contrast shows that predictability reduces instability, while unpredictability amplifies it. Systems with controlled variability maintain consistent load-capacity interaction, while systems with high variability experience frequent misalignment. Variability therefore is a key driver of pressure when not structurally contained.

Discretionary expenses function as adjustable load that can be increased, reduced, or removed in response to capacity conditions. This adjustability gives the system the ability to modify load dynamically, creating a mechanism for maintaining alignment.

This mechanism defines adjustable load as flexible demand. Unlike fixed or variable expenses, discretionary expenses can be altered without structural disruption. This allows the system to respond to changes in capacity by adjusting load, preventing pressure formation.

Over time, adjustable load provides a buffer against instability. When capacity decreases, discretionary expenses can be reduced, maintaining alignment. When capacity increases, they can expand without creating pressure. Stable systems use adjustable load to absorb fluctuations in capacity, preserving stability.

The contrast illustrates that systems without adjustable load lack the ability to respond to constraint. In such systems, all load behaves as fixed or variable, increasing pressure risk. Discretionary expenses therefore introduce flexibility that directly supports expense stability.

Adjustability determines the system's flexibility in managing load under changing capacity conditions. Systems with higher adjustability can reconfigure load to maintain alignment, reducing pressure formation. This flexibility is derived primarily from discretionary expenses.

This mechanism defines flexibility as the capacity to modify load structure. When load can be adjusted, the system can respond to capacity fluctuations without generating pressure. This ability transforms discretionary load into a stabilizing force within the system.

Over time, flexibility allows the system to adapt to both predictable and unpredictable changes in capacity. Stable systems maintain sufficient adjustable load to respond to disruptions, preserving alignment. Unstable systems lack this flexibility, causing load to remain fixed even when capacity declines.

The contrast shows that flexibility enables stability, while rigidity amplifies instability. Systems with high adjustability maintain control over load, preventing pressure accumulation. Systems with low adjustability experience persistent misalignment, reinforcing the importance of discretionary load in maintaining stability.

Expense composition represents the structural mix of fixed, variable, and discretionary load within the system. This composition determines how total load behaves under different conditions, influencing pressure formation and stability. It is not the total load but its composition that defines system behavior.

This mechanism defines composition as the arrangement of load types. Each category contributes differently to system dynamics: fixed load establishes baseline demand, variable load introduces fluctuation, and discretionary load provides adjustment capacity. The interaction of these elements determines overall stability.

Over time, composition shapes how the system responds to changes in capacity. Stable systems balance these categories, ensuring that baseline load remains absorbable, variability is controlled, and sufficient adjustability exists. Unstable systems exhibit imbalanced composition, such as excessive fixed load or insufficient discretionary capacity.

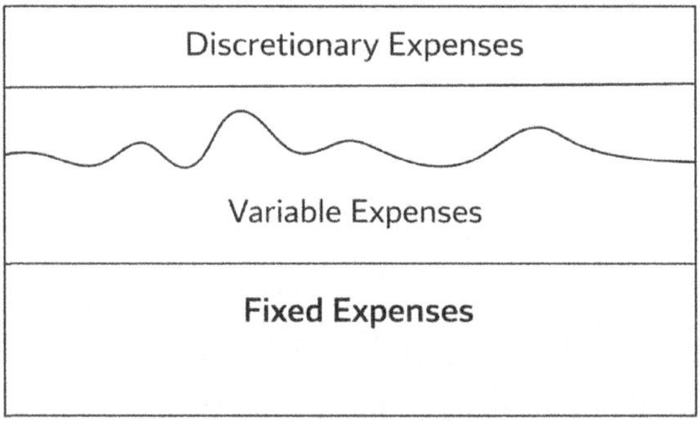

[Figure 3: Expense Categories — fixed vs variable vs discretionary layers]

The contrast demonstrates that composition governs system resilience. Two systems with identical total load can exhibit different stability outcomes based on their composition. Expense stability depends on how load is structured, not simply on how much load exists.

Systems with high fixed load operate under rigid conditions, while systems with higher flexible load maintain adaptive capacity. This distinction defines how systems respond to changes in capacity and how pressure forms under constraint.

This mechanism defines rigid systems as those dominated by fixed expenses, where baseline load consumes most available capacity. Flexible systems, by contrast, allocate a greater portion of load to adjustable categories, allowing dynamic response to capacity changes.

Over time, rigid systems experience persistent pressure when capacity declines because fixed load cannot adjust. Flexible systems reduce discretionary load to maintain alignment, preventing pressure accumulation. This difference determines how each system behaves under stress conditions.

The contrast highlights that rigidity increases instability, while flexibility enhances stability. High-fixed systems operate with limited margin for adjustment, making them vulnerable to pressure. High-flexible systems maintain the ability to reconfigure load, preserving alignment and reducing instability.

Each expense category responds differently when the system is under constraint. Fixed expenses maintain load regardless of capacity, variable expenses fluctuate but may still exceed capacity, and discretionary expenses can be adjusted to reduce load. These responses determine how pressure evolves.

This mechanism defines constraint response as category-specific behavior under limited capacity. Fixed load creates immediate pressure when capacity declines, variable load may either increase or decrease pressure depending on magnitude, and discretionary load provides the only direct means of reducing demand.

Over time, the interaction of these responses determines whether pressure accumulates or dissipates. Stable systems rely on discretionary adjustment to offset fixed and variable load, maintaining alignment. Unstable systems lack sufficient adjustable load, allowing pressure to persist.

The contrast shows that systems with balanced category responses can manage constraint effectively. Systems dominated by fixed and variable load without adjustability experience sustained pressure. Constraint response therefore is a function of composition, not individual expenses.

Total spend does not determine stability; load composition determines how that spend interacts with capacity. Two systems with identical total expenses can have different stability outcomes based on how those expenses are structured across categories.

This mechanism defines composition as the primary determinant of load behavior. Fixed, variable, and discretionary expenses interact differently with capacity, shaping how pressure forms. Total spend aggregates these effects but does not reveal their structure.

Over time, composition influences whether load remains aligned with capacity. Stable systems maintain compositions that allow consistent absorption and adjustment. Unstable systems may have manageable totals but poor composition, leading to misalignment and pressure.

The contrast demonstrates that evaluating totals without structure obscures system behavior. Stability emerges from how load is organized, not from how much is spent. Composition provides the framework for understanding this interaction.

Expense composition functions as the primary driver of system stability by determining how load behaves relative to capacity. The mix of fixed, variable, and discretionary expenses defines whether the system can maintain alignment over time.

This mechanism positions composition as the central determinant of resilience. Systems with balanced composition maintain baseline load within capacity, control variability, and retain sufficient adjustability. This structure prevents pressure from accumulating into stress.

Over time, composition governs how the system responds to changes in capacity and load conditions. Stable systems preserve alignment through structural balance, while unstable systems experience persistent misalignment due to poor composition.

The contrast reinforces that stability is not a function of magnitude but of structure. Expense composition defines how load interacts with capacity, making it the primary driver of system behavior.

The Baseline Cost of Living

Baseline load is the minimum persistent demand required for system operation. It represents the portion of expense load that remains across intervals and must be absorbed regardless of changing conditions. This establishes baseline as the minimum operating requirement within the system's current configuration. Stability begins with whether capacity can sustain this load continuously.

This mechanism defines baseline load as structural rather than descriptive. It is not the full expense profile or a summary of all outflow. It is the portion of load that persists before variability or adjustment enters the system. This distinction matters because baseline sets the minimum level of continuous demand the system must manage.

Over time, baseline load appears in every interval as recurring demand on capacity. Because it does not disappear between periods, it functions as the constant operating requirement beneath all other load behavior. Stable systems maintain baseline at a level that reliable capacity can absorb without compression. Unstable systems carry baseline too close to capacity, allowing pressure to form with minimal disturbance.

The contrast is foundational. A system with a clearly supportable baseline begins from structural stability, while a system with an oversized baseline begins from structural fragility. Baseline therefore defines the starting condition from which all other pressure dynamics emerge.

Baseline functions as the structural floor of the expense system. It establishes the lowest level of persistent load beneath which the system cannot operate without altering its configuration. This makes baseline the fixed operating platform on which all additional expense behavior is layered.

This mechanism defines the baseline floor as embedded in the arrangement of obligations rather than in temporary spending patterns. Fixed and non-eliminable expenses anchor that floor, creating continuous demand that capacity must meet before any variable or discretionary load is considered. The structural floor exists independently of short-term fluctuation.

Over time, the structural floor remains present in each interval, providing continuity but also imposing constraint. Stable systems maintain a floor that leaves meaningful room between baseline and capacity. Unstable systems operate with a floor set too high, reducing flexibility and increasing pressure sensitivity from the outset.

The contrast shows why the structural floor matters more than descriptive categories of spending. A lower, supportable floor preserves operating margin, while a high floor narrows the system's range of safe function. Baseline as structural floor therefore defines the lower boundary of stability.

Baseline load must be separated from total load because the system behaves differently at its minimum operating level than at its full expense profile. Total load includes all expenses applied across time, while baseline includes only the persistent portion required for continued operation. Stability is shaped first by what cannot be removed.

This mechanism defines baseline as a subset of total load with distinct structural significance. Total load changes as variable and discretionary components rise or fall, but baseline remains beneath those movements. The system's pressure condition depends heavily on how much of total load is fixed into this layer.

Over time, total load expands and contracts around the baseline floor. Stable systems may carry higher total load without instability if baseline remains well below capacity and variability is contained. Unstable systems may appear manageable in total terms but remain fragile because too much of that load is persistent.

The contrast is decisive. Total load describes the full demand profile, but baseline defines the minimum demand that cannot be escaped within the current structure. Stability depends less on total volume than on how much is embedded in baseline.

Baseline pressure forms when persistent load approaches or exceeds available capacity. Because baseline exists in every interval, the pressure associated with it is ongoing rather than episodic. It reflects the standing condition created by the system's minimum operating requirement.

This mechanism defines baseline pressure as the continuous burden produced by persistent load. When baseline remains comfortably below reliable capacity, that burden is absorbable. When baseline approaches capacity, ordinary operation begins to generate pressure.

Over time, baseline pressure establishes the background condition under which all other load is processed. Stable systems absorb it without significant compression, preserving room for fluctuation. Unstable systems absorb it narrowly, causing even minor additional load to exceed capacity.

The contrast is structural. In one case, baseline pressure remains contained within margin. In the other, it occupies most of the system's capacity, leaving little tolerance for change. Baseline pressure therefore determines whether the system begins from stability or near-instability.

Baseline load persists across time because it is present in every operating interval regardless of changing conditions. The system encounters it as recurring structural demand, not as a one-time event. That persistence makes baseline central to expense stability.

This mechanism defines persistence as continuous recurrence without discretionary reset. Baseline reasserts itself in each interval, requiring repeated absorption. The system cannot rely on periodic relief unless the structure changes.

Over time, persistent baseline shapes how all other expenses are experienced. Stable systems absorb it while preserving room for variation. Unstable systems begin each interval under compression because baseline remains too close to capacity.

The contrast shows why persistence matters more than simple presence. Temporary load can dissipate, but baseline reappears before the system can reset. Baseline persistence defines the system's starting pressure condition in every interval.

Operating margin is the distance between baseline load and available capacity. This distance determines how much room exists to absorb additional load without generating pressure. It is a structural measure of separation between minimum demand and absorptive ability.

This mechanism defines operating margin as usable space above baseline. When capacity exceeds baseline meaningfully, the system can process variability and timing shifts without instability. When the distance is narrow, the system operates close to its floor and becomes highly sensitive to pressure.

Over time, operating margin acts as the buffer within which ordinary variation can be absorbed. Stable systems preserve sufficient distance from baseline. Unstable systems maintain minimal distance, so small fluctuations quickly create pressure.

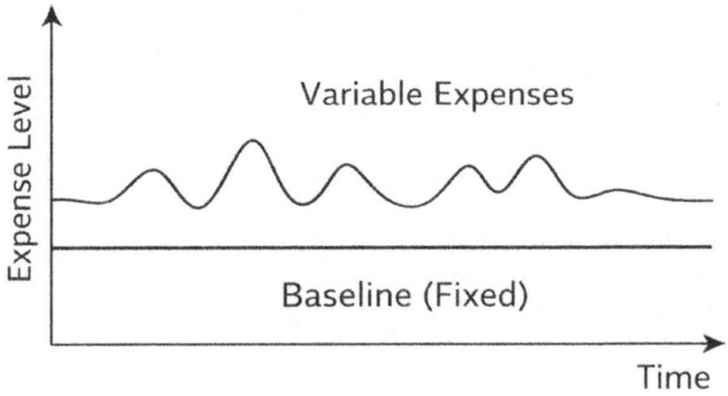

[Figure 4: Baseline Cost Structure — minimum expense level with variability above]

The contrast is clear. A wide margin allows stability under routine variation, while a compressed margin forces operation near constraint. Distance from baseline defines the space within which stability can be maintained.

Margin compression occurs when baseline rises relative to capacity, reducing the operating space above the structural floor. This does not simply increase demand; it narrows the system's ability to absorb fluctuation. As baseline approaches capacity, tolerance declines.

This mechanism defines compression as the shrinkage of the gap between baseline and capacity. As the gap narrows, additional load translates into pressure more quickly. Capacity becomes increasingly committed to persistent demand, leaving less available for variability or timing mismatch.

Over time, compressed margin changes system behavior. Stable systems with wider margin absorb fluctuation without persistent stress. Unstable systems with compressed margin experience stress from small deviations because variation occurs too close to the system's limit.

The contrast shows that compression is a structural narrowing of the stable operating zone. It transforms ordinary load movement into a greater source of pressure and increases the likelihood of instability.

Variability operates above baseline because fluctuations occur on top of minimum persistent demand. Baseline forms the fixed floor, while variable and adjustable components rise and fall above it. The system absorbs variability only after baseline has already consumed part of capacity.

This mechanism defines variability as additive. The system first carries baseline, then processes fluctuation. The effect of variability depends on how much capacity remains after baseline is covered.

Over time, this layering changes how the same fluctuation is experienced. Stable systems with lower baseline can absorb swings because margin remains. Unstable systems with high baseline experience the same swings as immediate pressure.

The contrast is structural. Variability does not operate independently; its effect depends on the baseline beneath it. This explains why identical fluctuations can be stable in one system and destabilizing in another.

High-baseline systems and low-baseline systems behave differently because the structural floor determines available flexibility. A high-baseline system commits much of capacity to persistent demand before additional load appears. A low-baseline system leaves a wider range for absorbing variation.

This mechanism defines high-baseline systems as structurally rigid and low-baseline systems as structurally flexible. In high-baseline systems, fixed demand consumes most capacity. In low-baseline systems, persistent demand remains lighter relative to capacity.

Over time, these configurations produce different pressure behaviors. Low-baseline systems process changes without frequent pressure formation. High-baseline systems experience recurrent compression because modest changes push load beyond capacity.

The contrast shows that baseline height is structural, not descriptive. Low-baseline systems preserve resilience through distance from constraint, while high-baseline systems operate close to their limit.

Pressure sensitivity increases when the system operates too close to baseline because the remaining distance to capacity is narrow. In that condition, small changes in load or timing produce large stability effects.

This mechanism defines pressure sensitivity as responsiveness to small disturbances when margin is compressed. Systems with wide margin absorb minor deviations. Systems near baseline-capacity proximity cannot, because even small changes exceed absorptive range.

Over time, high sensitivity produces frequent stress from routine movement. Stable systems remain relatively insensitive. Unstable systems react to minor changes, causing pressure to appear repeatedly.

The contrast is decisive. One system requires significant disruption to destabilize, while the other requires very little. The closer baseline sits to capacity, the less disturbance is needed to create pressure.

Baseline is a structural condition, not a behavioral description. It emerges from persistent obligations and non-eliminable requirements. The system responds to what is structurally present, not to interpretation.

This mechanism defines structural baseline as the arrangement of expenses that remain active across intervals. Once embedded, it functions as an operating fact. Its effect is determined by its relation to capacity.

Over time, baseline reproduces automatically as long as the structure remains intact. Stable systems maintain a baseline that capacity can support without compression. Unstable systems operate with a baseline that continually presses against capacity.

The contrast clarifies the boundary. Behavioral explanations focus on decisions, while structural explanations focus on configuration. Baseline belongs to the latter.

Baseline functions as a stability constraint because it defines the minimum load that must be absorbed before additional demand can be tolerated. It establishes the boundary within which stability operates.

This mechanism defines constraint as the point at which persistent demand limits flexibility. A low baseline preserves capacity for variation. A high baseline narrows that space.

Over time, baseline constraint shapes the entire pressure environment. Stable systems remain clear of the constraint boundary. Unstable systems operate near it, causing small disturbances to produce repeated pressure.

The contrast captures the core point. Baseline is the limiting floor that determines how much instability the system can tolerate. It is a defining constraint on expense stability.

Expense Variability and Instability

Expense variability is the fluctuation of load in magnitude and timing across intervals. It represents how applied demand deviates from a stable, predictable pattern. This separates variability from total load and baseline, positioning it as a structural modifier of load behavior rather than load size.

This mechanism defines variability as time-based deviation from consistent load application. When expenses change in size or occur irregularly, the system experiences variation in its demand profile, altering how load interacts with capacity.

Over time, variability introduces dynamic changes in the load profile. Stable systems maintain bounded variability within capacity. Unstable systems exhibit fluctuations that exceed capacity at specific intervals, creating localized pressure.

The contrast is structural. Low variability produces predictable interaction with capacity, while high variability creates uneven demand and higher pressure risk.

Magnitude variability refers to changes in load size across intervals. It occurs when the amount applied in one period differs from another, creating uneven demand.

This mechanism defines magnitude variability as amplitude change. Larger swings increase the likelihood that load exceeds capacity at certain intervals. Even with stable averages, large deviations create pressure spikes.

Over time, magnitude variability produces alternating periods of lower and higher demand. Stable systems keep fluctuations within absorbable range. Unstable systems experience shifts that exceed capacity and generate pressure.

The contrast shows that size variation is a major instability source. Controlled variation maintains alignment, while extreme variation creates repeated imbalance.

Timing variability refers to irregular sequencing of load across intervals. It occurs when expenses are not applied in consistent patterns, causing misalignment between load timing and capacity availability.

This mechanism defines timing variability as sequencing inconsistency. Even with stable magnitude, irregular timing can cluster load, increasing the likelihood that capacity is unavailable when needed.

Over time, timing variability disrupts alignment. Stable systems maintain consistent sequencing. Unstable systems experience repeated mismatches between load and capacity.

The contrast shows that timing alone can drive instability. Predictable sequencing preserves continuity, while irregular timing produces frequent misalignment.

Variability can create instability even when total load remains moderate because instability depends on distribution across time, not aggregate amounts.

This mechanism defines independence from totals as a core property. Fluctuations can exceed capacity at specific intervals even when overall load is manageable.

Over time, identical totals produce different outcomes depending on variability. Stable systems distribute load evenly. Unstable systems concentrate or irregularly apply load, creating pressure.

The contrast shows that totals alone cannot explain system behavior. Variability determines whether load stays within capacity at each interval.

Controlled variation represents bounded fluctuation, while volatility represents unbounded and unpredictable fluctuation. The distinction determines whether variability remains absorbable.

This mechanism defines controlled variation as fluctuation within limits. These limits allow capacity to anticipate and absorb changes. Volatility lacks such limits, producing irregular spikes.

Over time, controlled variation maintains alignment. Volatility produces repeated pressure events by exceeding capacity unpredictably.

The contrast shows that variability is not inherently destabilizing. When bounded, it supports stability. When unbounded, it drives instability.

Variability contributes to pressure by increasing the frequency of intervals in which load exceeds capacity. These imbalances arise from fluctuations in magnitude or timing.

This mechanism defines variability as a trigger for localized pressure. Each excessive fluctuation creates a point of imbalance, even if averages remain stable.

Over time, repeated variability-driven pressure leads to stress. Stable systems limit such events. Unstable systems experience them frequently.

The contrast shows that fluctuating load—not just high load—drives pressure formation.

Variability operates above baseline, interacting with the persistent load floor. All fluctuations occur after baseline has already consumed part of capacity.

This mechanism defines variability as additive to baseline. The system first absorbs baseline, then processes fluctuation. High baseline leaves less room for variability.

Over time, this interaction determines stability. Systems with sufficient margin absorb variability. Systems with compressed margin experience pressure from even moderate changes.

The contrast shows that variability must be evaluated relative to baseline.

Variability degrades predictability by making load behavior harder to anticipate. Irregular magnitude or timing reduces the system's ability to align capacity with demand.

This mechanism defines predictability as consistency of load patterns. As variability increases, predictability declines, increasing misalignment risk.

Over time, reduced predictability leads to repeated pressure. Stable systems maintain consistent patterns. Unstable systems experience irregular demand that prevents alignment.

The contrast shows that predictability stabilizes the system.

Variability disrupts continuity by breaking consistent alignment between load and capacity. Irregular demand prevents smooth operation.

This mechanism defines continuity as uninterrupted alignment. Variability breaks this alignment, creating pressure.

Over time, repeated disruptions accumulate into instability. Stable systems maintain continuity. Unstable systems experience frequent breakdowns.

The contrast shows that continuity is essential for stability.

Variability increases sensitivity to shock by reducing available capacity at certain intervals. Fluctuating load leaves less room for unexpected disturbances.

This mechanism defines sensitivity as responsiveness to external shocks. High variability creates periods where capacity is already stressed, amplifying shock impact.

Over time, high-variability systems experience stronger disruption from shocks. Stable systems preserve capacity to absorb them.

The contrast shows that variability amplifies shock effects when uncontrolled.

Stable variability systems maintain bounded, predictable fluctuations. Unstable systems exhibit irregular and excessive variability.

This mechanism defines stability in terms of variability structure. Stable systems operate within absorbable ranges. Unstable systems exceed them.

Over time, stable systems preserve continuity, while unstable systems experience repeated pressure and stress.

The contrast shows that variability structure determines system behavior.

Variability functions as a primary driver of instability by disrupting alignment between load and capacity. Fluctuations create repeated pressure events that accumulate into stress.

This mechanism positions variability as a structural source of instability. Even with stable baseline and totals, variability can introduce imbalance.

Over time, high variability leads to continuous pressure accumulation. Controlled variability prevents this.

The contrast reinforces that unbounded variability drives instability, while bounded variability preserves stability.

Expense Pressure and System Stress

Expense pressure is the condition in which load exceeds capacity at the point of interaction. It represents the immediate imbalance between applied demand and available absorptive ability. This definition establishes pressure as a mechanical output of load-capacity interaction, not a descriptive or subjective state. Whenever outflow surpasses inflow and accessible liquidity within an interval, pressure is created.

This mechanism defines pressure as instantaneous and interval-specific. It occurs at the exact moment the system cannot fully absorb applied load. The system does not average conditions at the point of interaction; it responds to immediate imbalance. Pressure therefore serves as a precise signal of misalignment between load and capacity.

Over time, pressure may appear intermittently or persist depending on how often load exceeds capacity. Stable systems experience limited, isolated pressure events that are resolved within the same interval. Unstable systems encounter frequent or sustained pressure, indicating recurring misalignment.

The contrast is structural. In one case, pressure is contained and temporary, with capacity restoring alignment quickly. In the other, pressure appears repeatedly or continuously, signaling that load exceeds capacity as a persistent condition. Expense pressure therefore marks the immediate boundary between alignment and imbalance.

Pressure must be understood as time-dependent rather than as a single event. While it is generated at specific moments of imbalance, its significance depends on how it behaves across intervals. The system does not interpret pressure in isolation; it evaluates whether it persists, repeats, or dissipates.

This mechanism defines temporal pressure as imbalance extending beyond a single interval. A single instance of load exceeding capacity may be absorbed without lasting effect. When pressure repeats or remains unresolved, it becomes a continuous condition rather than an isolated occurrence.

Over time, the frequency and duration of pressure events determine system behavior. Stable systems resolve pressure quickly, preventing carryover. Unstable systems allow pressure to persist or recur, creating sustained imbalance.

The contrast highlights the role of time. Event-based analysis captures isolated imbalance, while time-based analysis captures persistence. Pressure as a time-dependent condition therefore shifts focus to continuous system behavior.

Sustained load creates continuous pressure when persistent demand exceeds capacity across multiple intervals. This occurs when baseline load or recurring outflows remain too high relative to inflow and liquidity. Pressure then becomes a standing condition rather than an occasional event.

This mechanism defines continuous pressure as persistent load exceeding capacity without resolution. The system does not return to alignment between intervals because the underlying condition remains unchanged. Each interval begins with imbalance already present.

Over time, continuous pressure prevents recovery and increases system stress. Stable systems maintain sustained load within capacity. Unstable systems carry sustained load that exceeds capacity, creating constant imbalance.

The contrast shows that sustained load determines whether pressure becomes structural. When persistent demand is absorbable, pressure remains temporary. When it is not, pressure becomes continuous.

Pressure accumulates when imbalance is not resolved within the interval in which it occurs and carries forward. This accumulation represents unmet demand that increases total system stress. The system retains the effects of prior imbalance rather than resetting.

This mechanism defines accumulation as the persistence of unmet demand across intervals. Each instance of excess load adds to a backlog that must be absorbed. Accumulated pressure compounds, making future alignment more difficult.

Over time, accumulation transforms discrete pressure events into sustained stress. Stable systems prevent accumulation by resolving imbalance within each interval. Unstable systems allow pressure to carry forward, compounding stress.

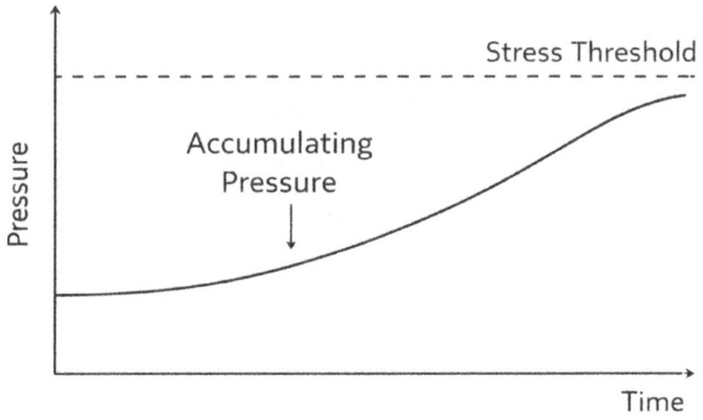

[Figure 5: Expense Pressure Over Time — sustained load buildup]

The contrast shows that accumulation marks the transition from temporary imbalance to structural instability. Contained pressure dissipates; accumulated pressure persists and intensifies.

System stress is the accumulation of pressure across multiple intervals. It represents the structural condition that develops when repeated or sustained imbalance is not resolved. Stress is cumulative rather than event-based.

This mechanism defines stress as the aggregation of unresolved pressure. Each instance of imbalance contributes to overall stress, which becomes embedded in system behavior.

Over time, stress alters how the system responds to load. Stable systems prevent stress by resolving pressure quickly. Unstable systems allow pressure to persist, causing stress to build.

The contrast clarifies that pressure is immediate and interval-based, while stress is cumulative and structural. Stress represents the long-term consequence of repeated imbalance.

The transition from pressure to stress occurs when imbalance persists across intervals and begins to accumulate. This marks the shift from temporary misalignment to structural stress.

This mechanism defines the transition as a threshold of accumulation. When pressure is resolved quickly, it remains isolated. When it repeats or persists, it accumulates and becomes stress.

Over time, this transition depends on the frequency and duration of pressure events. Stable systems remain below the threshold. Unstable systems exceed it, allowing stress to compound.

The contrast shows that the transition is progressive rather than binary. Systems move from isolated pressure to accumulated stress through repeated imbalance.

System tolerance declines as stress accumulates, reducing the system's ability to absorb additional load without generating further pressure. Tolerance represents remaining absorptive capacity before breakdown.

This mechanism defines tolerance as a function of accumulated stress. Each instance of unresolved pressure reduces the system's ability to absorb future load, increasing sensitivity to imbalance.

Over time, reduced tolerance amplifies instability. Stable systems maintain high tolerance by preventing accumulation. Unstable systems experience declining tolerance, making even small increases generate pressure.

The contrast highlights that tolerance is dynamic. Systems with low stress retain capacity, while stressed systems lose it.

Sustained pressure produces compounding effects as repeated imbalance increases stress at an accelerating rate. Each unresolved interval adds to existing stress, amplifying instability.

This mechanism defines compounding as nonlinear accumulation of pressure. As stress increases, each additional instance has greater impact, further reducing absorptive capacity.

Over time, compounding transforms moderate instability into severe stress. Stable systems prevent compounding by resolving pressure early. Unstable systems allow escalation.

The contrast shows that compounding drives rapid deterioration when pressure is not contained.

Recovery occurs when pressure is resolved and the system returns to alignment, while persistent stress occurs when pressure remains unresolved and continues to accumulate.

This mechanism defines recovery as dissipation of pressure within or between intervals. When capacity absorbs load and eliminates imbalance, the system resets. Persistent stress reflects continued accumulation without resolution.

Over time, recovery preserves stability by preventing stress formation. Stable systems resolve pressure quickly. Unstable systems fail to recover, allowing stress to grow.

The contrast shows that recovery is conditional, not automatic. Persistent stress indicates that alignment has not been restored.

Stress degrades effective capacity by reducing the system's ability to absorb load. As stress accumulates, resources such as liquidity are consumed, diminishing absorptive ability.

This mechanism defines capacity degradation as erosion under sustained stress. As stress increases, less capacity remains available, making further pressure more likely.

Over time, degraded capacity leads to more frequent and severe pressure events. Stable systems preserve capacity by avoiding stress. Unstable systems experience declining capacity.

The contrast shows that capacity is dynamic. Systems that preserve it remain stable; those that degrade it become increasingly unstable.

Stable systems contain pressure within manageable limits, while stressed systems accumulate pressure into structural stress. This distinction defines whether the system operates within capacity or exceeds it over time.

This mechanism defines stability as containment and stress as accumulation. Stable systems resolve pressure without buildup. Stressed systems allow pressure to persist.

Over time, stable systems maintain alignment and capacity. Stressed systems experience declining tolerance and increasing pressure frequency.

The contrast shows that stability and stress are processes. Systems move toward stability by resolving pressure and toward stress by accumulating it.

Stress functions as the precursor to system breakdown by representing accumulated imbalance that precedes failure. When stress exceeds remaining tolerance, the system transitions into breakdown.

This mechanism defines breakdown as the point where accumulated stress exceeds absorptive capacity. At this stage, pressure cannot be contained without structural change.

Over time, systems approach breakdown through stress accumulation. Stable systems prevent this progression. Unstable systems move toward breakdown as stress compounds.

The contrast shows that breakdown is gradual, not sudden. It is the result of sustained stress rather than isolated events.

Expense Inflation and Drift

Expense drift is the gradual increase in baseline load over time. It represents a structural expansion of the system's minimum operating requirement without a single defining event. Drift is therefore cumulative rather than discrete.

This mechanism defines drift as incremental baseline movement. Each adjustment may be small in isolation, but collectively they raise the required load floor. Because baseline persists, any increase becomes embedded in every future interval.

Over time, drift changes how load interacts with capacity by increasing minimum demand. Stable systems maintain baseline growth at a rate capacity can match. Unstable systems allow baseline to rise faster than capacity, reducing margin.

The contrast shows that drift is not visible in single intervals. Stable systems maintain consistent baseline relative to capacity, while drifting systems experience gradual compression of stability.

Drift differs from discrete change in that it occurs incrementally rather than suddenly. A discrete change introduces a noticeable shift at a specific moment, while drift consists of small adjustments that accumulate.

This mechanism defines discrete change as event-based and drift as process-based. Discrete increases are immediately observable. Drift operates below detection thresholds, gradually altering baseline.

Over time, discrete changes produce immediate pressure shifts, while drift increases pressure risk gradually. Stable systems can absorb discrete changes if capacity remains aligned. Drift alters structure continuously.

The contrast shows that discrete changes are visible and bounded, while drift is gradual and persistent. Systems may adapt to sudden increases but remain vulnerable to slow expansion.

Baseline expansion occurs when persistent load increases structurally, raising the system's minimum requirement. Each addition becomes part of the baseline and persists across intervals.

This mechanism defines expansion as incorporation of additional load into the baseline layer. Unlike variability, which fluctuates above baseline, expansion raises the baseline itself.

Over time, expansion reduces flexibility. Stable systems limit expansion to preserve margin. Unstable systems experience ongoing expansion that narrows the gap between baseline and capacity.

The contrast shows that expansion alters structure rather than temporary demand.

Drift operates as a continuous process because baseline adjustments accumulate across intervals. Each increase becomes embedded and carried forward.

This mechanism defines drift as persistent structural change. The system does not reset; it inherits the expanded baseline each interval.

Over time, continuous drift alters system equilibrium. Stable systems experience minimal drift. Unstable systems exhibit ongoing expansion that reduces stability.

The contrast shows that drift is not episodic but continuous.

Drift is often hidden because its incremental nature makes individual changes difficult to detect. Each increase may appear insignificant, but their cumulative effect is substantial.

This mechanism defines hidden change as accumulation below perceptual thresholds. Without a defining event, drift is not immediately identified as a source of pressure.

Over time, hidden drift delays recognition of instability. Stable systems monitor baseline relative to capacity. Unstable systems allow unnoticed expansion.

The contrast shows that visibility determines response.

Drift compresses margin by raising baseline closer to capacity. As baseline increases, the distance to capacity decreases, limiting the ability to absorb additional load.

This mechanism defines margin compression as narrowing of absorptive space. Each increase reduces room for variability and temporary demand.

Over time, compression increases pressure likelihood. Stable systems preserve margin. Unstable systems experience progressive compression.

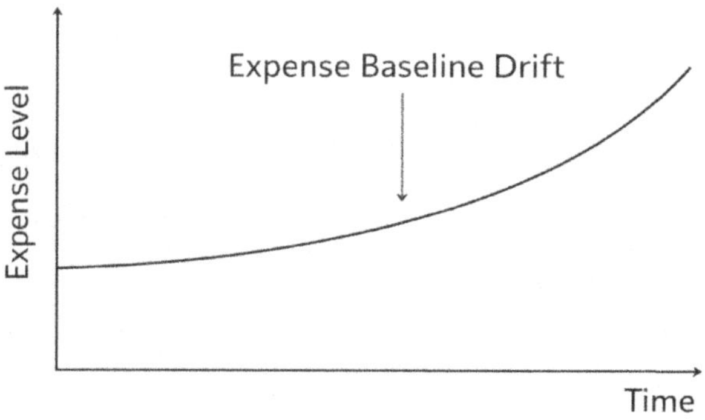

[Figure 6: Expense Drift — rising baseline over time]

The contrast shows that margin determines stability tolerance.

Drift contributes to pressure growth by increasing baseline without corresponding capacity growth. As baseline rises, the system operates closer to its limit.

This mechanism defines pressure growth as increasing imbalance risk. Drift raises the probability of pressure without discrete events.

Over time, drift-induced pressure becomes persistent. Stable systems maintain alignment. Unstable systems allow baseline to exceed capacity.

The contrast shows that pressure can increase without visible triggers.

Drift differs from variability in that it affects baseline rather than fluctuations. Variability changes load above baseline, while drift raises the baseline itself.

This mechanism defines drift as baseline movement and variability as fluctuation. Variability is temporary; drift is structural.

Over time, variability produces intermittent pressure, while drift produces sustained pressure growth.

The contrast shows that drift is deeper and more structural than variability.

Drift differs from shock in that it is gradual, while shock is sudden. Shock introduces immediate change; drift unfolds incrementally.

This mechanism defines shock as abrupt disruption and drift as gradual transformation.

Over time, shocks create acute pressure that may dissipate. Drift creates chronic pressure by raising baseline continuously.

The contrast shows that shock and drift are distinct pathways to instability.

Drift compounds as each incremental increase adds to previous increases. Small changes accumulate into significant structural shifts.

This mechanism defines compounding as cumulative growth of baseline. Each increase builds on prior ones, raising required capacity.

Over time, compounding transforms minor drift into major instability. Stable systems limit expansion. Unstable systems allow continued growth.

The contrast shows that compounding magnifies small changes.

Stable systems maintain relatively constant baseline, while drift-dominated systems experience continuous expansion. This determines whether margin is preserved or eroded.

This mechanism defines drift-dominated systems as those with ongoing baseline increase. Stable systems maintain baseline within capacity.

Over time, stable systems preserve structure. Drift-dominated systems lose stability through continuous change.

The contrast shows that stability requires structural consistency.

Drift functions as a primary long-term driver of instability by raising baseline and reducing margin over time. This occurs without discrete events, making it persistent and often unnoticed.

This mechanism defines drift as cumulative structural change leading to instability. As baseline rises, pressure becomes more frequent.

Over time, drift reduces the ability to absorb variability and shocks. Stable systems prevent this through alignment. Unstable systems move toward breakdown as margin is exhausted.

The contrast shows that instability can emerge without sudden disruption. Gradual baseline expansion is sufficient to produce sustained pressure and stress.

Timing Mismatch in Expenses

Timing in expense systems is the sequencing of load and capacity across intervals. It determines when expenses are applied and when capacity becomes available to absorb them. This establishes timing as a structural variable governing interaction, not as a descriptive attribute of total flow. The system evaluates alignment at each interval based on sequence, not aggregate balance.

This mechanism defines timing as the order in which load and capacity meet. Load may be applied before, during, or after capacity becomes available, and each configuration produces a different outcome. The sequence of these interactions determines whether pressure forms at the point of application.

Over time, timing structures the interaction between inflow and outflow. Stable systems maintain sequencing in which capacity is available when load is applied, preserving alignment. Misaligned systems apply load before capacity arrives, creating immediate pressure even when total capacity is sufficient.

The contrast shows that timing is independent of magnitude. Systems with identical totals can exhibit stability or instability based solely on sequencing. Timing therefore determines whether load-capacity interaction produces continuity or pressure.

Timing functions as a structural variable because it governs alignment independent of magnitude. It is embedded in how the system operates across intervals, determining whether capacity is accessible when load is applied. This makes timing a core determinant of system behavior.

This mechanism defines timing as an ordering constraint within the system. The sequence in which inflow and outflow occur shapes how load is absorbed. Even when capacity equals or exceeds load in total, improper sequencing creates intervals in which capacity is unavailable, producing pressure.

Over time, timing influences the system's ability to maintain continuous alignment. Stable systems synchronize load application with capacity availability, ensuring consistent absorption. Misaligned systems experience recurring intervals in which load precedes capacity, generating repeated imbalance.

The contrast highlights that timing cannot be evaluated through totals. Systems with sufficient capacity may still experience instability if sequence is misaligned. Timing as a structural variable therefore determines whether the system operates smoothly or under repeated pressure.

Timing mismatch forms when load is applied before capacity becomes available within an interval. This misalignment creates a condition in which the system must absorb demand without sufficient resources at that moment. The mismatch is defined by sequence, not by insufficient total capacity.

This mechanism defines mismatch as a sequencing gap between load application and capacity availability. When expenses occur before income or liquidity is accessible, the system encounters immediate imbalance. The mismatch exists even if capacity arrives later within the same cycle.

Over time, timing mismatch produces repeated pressure if sequencing remains misaligned. Stable systems align load and capacity to minimize these occurrences. Misaligned systems experience persistent gaps, requiring continuous adjustment to maintain continuity.

The contrast shows that mismatch is not a function of magnitude. Systems with adequate total inflow may still experience instability because of sequence misalignment. Timing mismatch therefore represents a structural source of pressure independent of total resources.

Sequence gaps are intervals in which load occurs before capacity replenishment, creating a temporary absence of absorptive ability. These gaps are the precise points at which timing mismatch produces imbalance. The system must bridge them to maintain continuity.

This mechanism defines sequence gaps as temporal dislocations between demand and supply. When load is applied in advance of capacity, the system enters a state in which demand exceeds available resources. This gap persists until capacity becomes accessible.

Over time, repeated sequence gaps create recurring imbalance. Stable systems minimize or eliminate gaps by aligning inflow and outflow sequences. Misaligned systems experience frequent gaps, each representing a point of pressure formation.

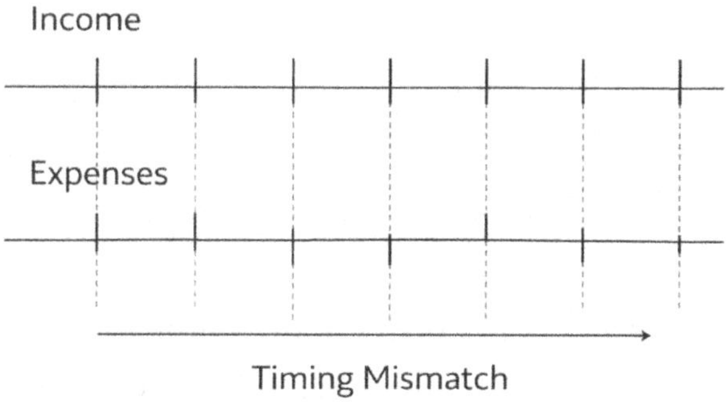

[Figure 7: Timing Mismatch — expense vs income misalignment]

The contrast shows that sequence gaps are the operational points of instability. Systems without gaps maintain continuous alignment, while systems with recurring gaps experience repeated pressure. Sequence gaps therefore represent the structural manifestation of timing mismatch.

Timing mismatch produces immediate pressure when load exceeds available capacity at the point of application. This pressure arises not from total insufficiency but from the absence of capacity at the required moment. The system responds to the sequence gap by generating imbalance.

This mechanism defines pressure formation as the direct result of sequencing failure. When capacity is delayed relative to load, the system cannot absorb demand, creating instantaneous pressure. Misalignment between inflow timing and outflow timing is sufficient to trigger imbalance.

Over time, repeated timing mismatch leads to frequent pressure events. Stable systems align sequencing to prevent these occurrences, maintaining continuous absorption. Misaligned systems experience pressure at each sequence gap, increasing the frequency of imbalance.

The contrast shows that pressure can arise even in systems with adequate resources. When timing is aligned, load is absorbed without issue. When timing is misaligned, pressure forms immediately. Timing mismatch therefore acts as a primary trigger of pressure independent of magnitude.

Total sufficiency of capacity does not prevent instability when timing is misaligned. A system may have enough income and liquidity in aggregate but still experience pressure because of sequence gaps. This distinction separates structural alignment from aggregate balance.

This mechanism defines sufficiency as inadequate when evaluated without timing. Total capacity must be available at the correct intervals to prevent pressure. When capacity arrives after load is applied, sufficiency in total does not eliminate imbalance at the point of interaction.

Over time, systems with sufficient totals but poor timing experience recurring pressure. Stable systems align inflow with outflow, ensuring that sufficiency translates into effective absorption. Misaligned systems fail to convert total capacity into usable capacity at the required moments.

The contrast demonstrates that aggregate measures obscure sequence-based instability. Systems with aligned timing maintain stability, while systems with misaligned timing experience pressure despite adequate totals. Timing therefore determines whether capacity sufficiency is operationally effective.

Repeated timing mismatch occurs when sequence gaps persist across multiple intervals, creating a structural pattern of misalignment. This repetition transforms isolated mismatch into a recurring condition that defines system behavior. The system repeatedly encounters intervals in which load precedes capacity.

This mechanism defines repetition as persistence of sequencing failure. Each interval reproduces the same misalignment, preventing the system from achieving continuous alignment. Repeated mismatch therefore becomes embedded in the system's structure.

Over time, repeated mismatch leads to frequent pressure events and may accumulate into stress. Stable systems correct sequencing to eliminate recurrence. Misaligned systems maintain the same sequence structure, causing ongoing imbalance.

The contrast highlights that repetition converts temporary mismatch into structural instability. Systems with isolated mismatch recover quickly, while systems with repeated mismatch experience sustained pressure. Repeated timing mismatch therefore defines long-term sequence-based instability.

Timing mismatch increases dependence on liquidity to bridge sequence gaps. When load is applied before capacity arrives, liquidity becomes the resource that absorbs load temporarily. This bridging function compensates for sequencing failure but introduces additional system dependency.

This mechanism defines liquidity dependence as the need to substitute immediate capacity for delayed inflow. Liquidity allows the system to maintain continuity during sequence gaps, but it is consumed in the process. That consumption reflects the cost of misalignment.

Over time, repeated reliance on liquidity reduces reserves and increases vulnerability. Stable systems minimize dependence by aligning timing. Misaligned systems require continuous bridging, leading to liquidity depletion and increased pressure.

The contrast shows that liquidity is not a solution but a compensatory mechanism. Systems with aligned timing preserve liquidity, while systems with persistent mismatch consume it. Timing mismatch therefore creates ongoing reliance on liquidity to maintain function.

Stable systems maintain synchronization between load and capacity, while misaligned systems operate with persistent sequence gaps. This distinction determines whether the system achieves continuous alignment or experiences recurring imbalance. Synchronization is the structural condition of stability.

This mechanism defines stable systems as those with aligned sequencing. Load is applied when capacity is available, preventing pressure formation. Misaligned systems apply load in advance of capacity, creating repeated imbalance.

Over time, stable systems sustain continuity through synchronized interaction. Misaligned systems experience frequent disruptions because of recurring gaps. This divergence leads to fundamentally different behaviors despite similar totals.

The contrast shows that synchronization determines system condition. Systems with aligned timing maintain stability, while systems with misalignment experience ongoing pressure. Timing alignment therefore defines whether the system operates smoothly or under stress.

Timing mismatch is distinct from variability because it relates to sequence rather than magnitude. Variability describes fluctuations in load size or distribution, while timing mismatch describes when load occurs relative to capacity. These mechanisms operate independently.

This mechanism defines timing as sequencing and variability as fluctuation. A system may have stable magnitude but misaligned timing, or variable magnitude with aligned timing. Each condition produces different effects on pressure formation.

Over time, variability creates pressure through magnitude changes, while timing mismatch creates pressure through sequencing gaps. Stable systems manage both by maintaining bounded variability and aligned timing. Unstable systems may experience instability from either or both mechanisms.

The contrast shows that timing and variability must be analyzed separately. Systems with controlled variability but poor timing still experience pressure. Timing mismatch therefore represents a distinct pathway to instability independent of load fluctuation.

Timing mismatch differs from drift because it involves sequence failure rather than gradual baseline increase. Drift raises the structural floor of load, while timing mismatch disrupts the alignment of load and capacity within intervals. These mechanisms affect stability differently.

This mechanism defines drift as structural expansion and timing mismatch as sequencing misalignment. Drift increases baseline pressure over time, while timing mismatch creates immediate pressure at specific intervals. The two can coexist but remain distinct.

Over time, drift produces gradual margin compression, while timing mismatch produces recurring gaps. Stable systems manage both by maintaining baseline alignment and synchronized sequencing. Unstable systems may experience compounded instability from both mechanisms.

The contrast highlights that drift alters long-term structure, while timing mismatch affects immediate interaction. Systems with stable baseline but poor timing still experience pressure. Timing mismatch therefore operates independently as a source of instability.

Timing functions as a core stability constraint because it determines whether load and capacity align at the moment of interaction. Without proper sequencing, even sufficient capacity cannot prevent pressure. This makes timing a fundamental requirement for system stability.

This mechanism defines timing as a constraint on effective capacity. Capacity must be available at the correct interval to absorb load. When sequence is misaligned, capacity becomes functionally unavailable despite its existence.

Over time, systems that maintain sequence alignment preserve stability, while systems with persistent mismatch experience recurring pressure. Stable systems treat timing as a structural condition, ensuring synchronization across intervals. Misaligned systems operate with ongoing sequence gaps, leading to instability.

The contrast reinforces that timing is not secondary to magnitude or composition. It is a primary determinant of whether the system can function without pressure. Timing therefore defines the boundary between effective capacity and operational imbalance.

Expense Shock and Sudden Load Increase

Expense shock is a discrete increase in load that occurs within a single interval, creating an abrupt surge in demand on the system. It is defined by its immediacy and magnitude relative to the existing load structure. Unlike baseline or variability, which operate across time, shock is concentrated at a specific point, producing immediate interaction with capacity. This establishes shock as an event-driven mechanism within an otherwise continuous system.

This mechanism defines shock as a sudden deviation from expected load patterns. It introduces demand that was not present in prior intervals and must be absorbed immediately. Because shock is not distributed across time, its full impact is concentrated at the moment of occurrence. This concentration distinguishes it from gradual or fluctuating load.

Over time, the effect of shock depends on how the system absorbs or fails to absorb the increase. Stable systems maintain sufficient margin and capacity to contain the event without sustained pressure. Unstable systems encounter immediate imbalance, generating pressure that may carry forward into stress.

The contrast is structural. In one case, shock is absorbed within existing capacity, preserving stability. In the other, shock exceeds capacity instantly, initiating imbalance. Expense shock therefore defines the system's response to abrupt load introduction.

Shock differs from continuous load in that it represents an abrupt increase rather than an ongoing demand. Continuous load is applied consistently across intervals, allowing capacity to align with persistent requirements. Shock disrupts this continuity by introducing sudden and concentrated demand.

This mechanism defines continuous load as predictable and distributed, while shock is immediate and concentrated. Continuous load allows the system to establish equilibrium over time. Shock interrupts that equilibrium by exceeding expected load levels within a single interval.

Over time, continuous load contributes to baseline and sustained pressure patterns, while shock introduces acute disruption. Stable systems maintain continuous load within capacity and absorb shocks without long-term imbalance. Unstable systems may manage continuous load but fail to absorb sudden spikes.

The contrast highlights that shock operates outside normal load patterns. Continuous load can be anticipated and aligned with capacity, while shock requires immediate absorption. Shock therefore represents a discontinuity in load behavior that tests structural resilience.

Shock differs from variability because it represents an unbounded spike rather than a bounded fluctuation. Variability involves changes in magnitude within a predictable or contained range, while shock introduces load that exceeds those bounds. This defines shock as a separate category of load behavior.

This mechanism defines variability as structured fluctuation and shock as structural discontinuity. Variability allows the system to anticipate and absorb changes within defined limits. Shock exceeds those limits, creating demand outside the system's expected range.

Over time, variability produces intermittent pressure when fluctuations exceed capacity, while shock produces immediate and often larger imbalance. Stable systems manage variability through margin, but shock tests whether that margin is sufficient for sudden demand.

The contrast shows that variability operates within the existing structure, while shock challenges that structure. Systems that handle variability may still be vulnerable to shock if margin is insufficient. Shock therefore represents an extreme deviation from normal fluctuation.

Shock differs from drift in that it is instantaneous rather than gradual. Drift increases baseline load incrementally across intervals, altering the system's structure over time. Shock introduces a sudden increase in load within a single interval without prior accumulation.

This mechanism defines drift as cumulative expansion and shock as discrete escalation. Drift reshapes baseline gradually, while shock creates immediate deviation from existing load. The system experiences drift as gradual compression and shock as abrupt disruption.

Over time, drift produces long-term pressure growth, while shock produces immediate pressure that may or may not persist. Stable systems manage drift through alignment with capacity and absorb shocks through available margin. Unstable systems may experience compounded effects when shock occurs on top of drift.

The contrast highlights that drift and shock represent different temporal patterns of instability. Drift operates slowly and continuously, while shock occurs suddenly and discretely. Shock therefore introduces immediate imbalance without the gradual buildup associated with drift.

Shock events form when a sudden increase in load is introduced within a single interval. This increase may arise from structural conditions that generate abrupt demand, such as concentrated obligations or external cost impositions. The defining characteristic is the immediacy of load application.

This mechanism defines shock formation as the concentration of load into a narrow time frame. Instead of being distributed across intervals, the load is applied all at once. This concentration intensifies interaction with capacity, increasing the likelihood of imbalance.

Over time, exposure to shock depends on how often such events occur and how they interact with existing load. Stable systems encounter shock events but absorb them without sustained disruption. Unstable systems experience repeated or poorly absorbed shocks, leading to pressure accumulation.

The contrast shows that shock formation is about structure, not randomness. Systems with concentrated load patterns are more susceptible to shock events, while distributed systems reduce the likelihood of abrupt spikes. Shock formation therefore reflects how load is organized over time.

Shock generates immediate pressure because the sudden increase in load exceeds available capacity at the point of occurrence. Unlike gradual or variable load, shock does not allow time for capacity adjustment. The system must respond instantly to the increased demand.

This mechanism defines immediate pressure as the direct result of abrupt imbalance. When shock occurs, capacity is evaluated at that moment, and any excess load creates pressure. There is no opportunity for sequencing or distribution to mitigate the effect.

Over time, the persistence of pressure depends on whether the system can absorb the shock within the same or subsequent intervals. Stable systems contain the pressure quickly, preventing accumulation. Unstable systems allow pressure to persist, contributing to stress.

The contrast illustrates that shock compresses time in the load-capacity interaction. Systems that can absorb sudden demand remain stable, while those that cannot experience immediate imbalance. Shock therefore represents a direct pathway to pressure formation.

Shock propagates through the system as the initial imbalance affects multiple components of capacity and structure. The sudden increase in load does not remain isolated; it transmits through liquidity use, alters subsequent intervals, and influences future load-capacity interaction. Propagation extends the impact of shock beyond the initial event.

This mechanism defines propagation as the spread of imbalance across system elements. When capacity is insufficient at the point of shock, the system compensates by drawing on liquidity or deferring load. This redistribution creates secondary effects that extend shock influence.

Over time, propagation determines whether shock remains isolated or becomes a source of ongoing stress. Stable systems contain propagation by absorbing the shock within existing capacity. Unstable systems experience extended effects as imbalance carries forward into future intervals.

The contrast shows that shock impact depends on containment. Systems that limit propagation return to alignment quickly, while systems that allow propagation experience prolonged instability. Shock propagation therefore defines how a single event influences system behavior over time.

Liquidity functions as the primary absorber of shock by providing immediate capacity to meet sudden load. When shock exceeds immediate inflow, liquidity bridges the gap between load and available resources. This positions liquidity as the system's first line of defense against abrupt imbalance.

This mechanism defines liquidity as accessible capacity that can be deployed instantly. Unlike income, which may be delayed, liquidity is available at the moment of shock. This immediacy allows the system to absorb load without generating sustained pressure.

Over time, liquidity use determines how shock affects future capacity. Stable systems use liquidity to absorb shock without significant reserve depletion. Unstable systems rely heavily on liquidity, reducing available capacity for future intervals and increasing vulnerability.

The contrast highlights that liquidity is a finite absorber. Systems with sufficient liquidity contain shocks effectively, while systems with limited liquidity experience immediate and persistent pressure. Liquidity therefore determines whether shock is absorbed or propagated.

Shock accelerates stress by compressing margin and increasing pressure within a single interval. The sudden increase in load reduces available capacity instantly, creating conditions in which pressure can accumulate into stress more rapidly than under gradual load changes. This acceleration distinguishes shock from other instability mechanisms.

This mechanism defines stress acceleration as rapid transition from pressure to stress. When shock generates significant imbalance, the system may not recover within the same interval. This allows pressure to carry forward, contributing to stress accumulation.

Over time, repeated or poorly absorbed shocks amplify stress. Stable systems limit acceleration by containing pressure quickly. Unstable systems experience compounding effects as each shock adds to existing stress.

The contrast shows that shock changes the rate of instability development. Gradual mechanisms build stress over time, while shock compresses that timeline. Shock-induced stress therefore represents an accelerated pathway to instability.

A single shock represents an isolated disruption, while repeated shocks form a pattern of recurring load spikes. This distinction determines whether the system experiences temporary imbalance or sustained instability. The frequency of shock events defines their cumulative impact.

This mechanism defines single shock as a discrete event and repeated shock as a structural pattern. A single event may be absorbed without lasting effect if capacity is sufficient. Repeated shocks introduce continuous disruption, preventing the system from stabilizing.

Over time, repeated shocks increase pressure frequency and contribute to stress accumulation. Stable systems absorb isolated shocks and maintain alignment. Unstable systems experience recurring shocks that compound imbalance.

The contrast highlights that frequency transforms impact. Systems that handle isolated shocks remain stable, while systems exposed to repeated shocks develop persistent stress. Repeated shock therefore converts discrete events into ongoing instability.

Shock can destabilize a system even in the absence of prior drift. A system with stable baseline and sufficient margin may still experience imbalance if a sudden load increase exceeds capacity. This demonstrates that shock operates independently of gradual structural change.

This mechanism defines independence as the ability of shock to create instability without prior baseline expansion. Even well-aligned systems are vulnerable if shock magnitude exceeds available capacity. The absence of drift does not eliminate exposure to sudden imbalance.

Over time, systems with stable structure recover from shock more effectively than systems already under stress. Stable systems absorb or dissipate pressure quickly, while unstable systems experience prolonged effects because of limited margin.

The contrast shows that drift and shock are separate pathways to instability. Drift creates gradual pressure, while shock creates immediate imbalance. Shock without prior drift therefore highlights the role of sudden events in system behavior.

Shock functions as an instability trigger by introducing immediate load that exceeds capacity, initiating pressure and potentially stress. It represents the point at which a system transitions from alignment to imbalance because of sudden demand. This makes shock a critical mechanism in system dynamics.

This mechanism defines shock as the initiator of instability events. When load increases abruptly, the system's ability to absorb demand is tested. If capacity is insufficient, pressure forms instantly, beginning the process of stress accumulation.

Over time, the outcome of shock depends on the system's ability to contain its effects. Stable systems absorb and resolve imbalance, preventing escalation. Unstable systems allow pressure to persist, leading to stress and potential breakdown.

The contrast reinforces that shock is not merely a disturbance but a structural test of resilience. Systems with sufficient capacity and margin withstand shock, while those without transition into instability. Shock therefore defines the entry point into sudden system stress.

Runaway Spending and Feedback Loops

Feedback in expense systems operates as a structural mechanism in which system output influences future input, creating a loop between load and subsequent load generation. This defines feedback as an internal dynamic rather than an external addition to demand. The system does not simply process load; under feedback conditions, it produces conditions that increase future load.

This mechanism establishes feedback as recursive interaction within the system. When applied load alters structure or conditions in a way that leads to additional load, a loop is formed. That loop can either stabilize or amplify system behavior depending on how output feeds back into input. In expense systems, the focus is on reinforcing loops that increase load.

Over time, feedback loops determine whether load remains bounded or begins to escalate. Stable systems exhibit neutral or balancing feedback, in which output does not significantly increase future demand. Unstable systems exhibit reinforcing feedback, in which each iteration increases load magnitude.

The contrast is structural. Systems without feedback process load linearly, while systems with feedback generate additional load from prior output. Feedback therefore introduces a mechanism by which the system becomes self-influencing, altering its own future demand conditions.

Non-linear load growth emerges when increases in load do not follow proportional relationships but instead accelerate over time. Linear growth represents direct, proportional increase in load relative to system inputs. Non-linear growth, by contrast, reflects compounding or accelerating increase driven by internal dynamics.

This mechanism defines linear growth as additive and predictable, while non-linear growth is multiplicative and accelerating. In linear systems, each increment of load produces a similar increment in future load. In non-linear systems, each increment produces a larger subsequent increase, amplifying demand.

Over time, linear growth allows capacity to adjust predictably, maintaining alignment if capacity expands proportionally. Non-linear growth challenges this alignment because load increases faster than capacity can respond. This divergence leads to pressure formation even if initial conditions appear stable.

The contrast shows that proportional systems remain controllable, while accelerating systems move toward instability. Non-linear growth introduces curvature into load progression, where each interval produces a larger increase than the previous one. This mechanism defines how feedback transforms steady demand into escalating pressure.

Reinforcing systems differ structurally because they amplify load through feedback, while stabilizing systems maintain equilibrium by neutralizing change. Reinforcing systems produce output that increases future input, creating escalation. Stabilizing systems produce output that counteracts change, preserving alignment between load and capacity.

This mechanism defines reinforcing feedback as positive amplification and stabilizing feedback as neutral or negative regulation. In reinforcing systems, each cycle increases load magnitude or frequency. In stabilizing systems, output does not generate additional demand, preventing escalation.

Over time, reinforcing systems exhibit expanding load trajectories, while stabilizing systems maintain bounded behavior. Stable systems contain feedback within limits that prevent amplification. Unstable systems allow reinforcing loops to dominate, leading to continuous load growth.

The contrast highlights that system behavior is determined by feedback structure. Systems with stabilizing feedback remain within capacity limits, while systems with reinforcing feedback exceed them. Reinforcing versus stabilizing dynamics therefore define whether feedback contributes to stability or instability.

Feedback loops form when system outputs alter conditions in a way that increases future load inputs. This requires a structural pathway through which output influences subsequent demand. The presence of such a pathway allows the system to become self-reinforcing rather than externally driven.

This mechanism defines loop formation as the connection between output and input. When applied load changes system conditions—such as reducing available capacity or increasing recurring obligations—it creates conditions for additional load. This linkage completes the loop.

Over time, feedback loops strengthen as repeated cycles reinforce the connection between output and input. Stable systems limit or interrupt this connection, preventing escalation. Unstable systems maintain or amplify it, allowing each cycle to increase load further.

The contrast shows that loop formation is structural rather than incidental. Systems without feedback pathways remain externally driven, while systems with such pathways generate internal escalation. Feedback loop formation therefore marks the transition from passive load processing to active load generation.

Spending as self-reinforcing load occurs when applied demand creates conditions that lead to additional demand in subsequent intervals. This transforms load from a static input into a dynamic process that generates further load. The system begins to produce its own increasing demand.

This mechanism defines self-reinforcement as load generating future load. When current expenses alter the system in a way that increases baseline, variability, or recurring obligations, they create new load that persists. This establishes a cycle of escalating demand.

Over time, self-reinforcing load produces compounding increases in system demand. Stable systems prevent this mechanism by maintaining separation between output and future input. Unstable systems allow output to feed directly into future load, creating continuous escalation.

The contrast shows that not all load is independent. In stable systems, load remains externally defined and bounded. In self-reinforcing systems, load becomes internally generated, increasing with each cycle. Spending as self-reinforcing load therefore defines the mechanism through which demand expands autonomously.

Escalation through internal dynamics occurs when load growth is driven by the system's own structure rather than by external inputs. This distinguishes feedback-driven growth from increases caused by external change. The system becomes the source of its own expansion.

This mechanism defines internal escalation as self-generated growth. When feedback loops exist, each cycle of load application modifies the system in a way that increases subsequent demand. This creates a closed-loop process in which escalation continues without external triggers.

Over time, internally driven escalation produces sustained load growth that may outpace capacity. Stable systems limit internal dynamics by maintaining boundaries that prevent feedback amplification. Unstable systems allow these dynamics to operate unchecked, leading to accelerating demand.

The contrast shows that externally driven systems respond to change, while internally driven systems generate it. Internal escalation introduces autonomy into load growth, making it independent of external conditions. This mechanism therefore defines how systems can become unstable without external shocks or drift.

Positive feedback loop mechanics describe how each cycle of load application increases the magnitude or frequency of subsequent load. This amplification occurs through the reinforcing connection between output and input. Each iteration strengthens the loop, increasing its effect on system behavior.

This mechanism defines positive feedback as exponential amplification. As load increases, it produces conditions that further increase load, creating a cycle of accelerating growth. The system does not stabilize between cycles; it intensifies.

Over time, positive feedback leads to rapid escalation in demand. Stable systems interrupt or dampen this amplification, preventing runaway growth. Unstable systems allow positive feedback to operate continuously, causing load to expand at an increasing rate.

The contrast shows that positive feedback alters the trajectory of load growth. Systems without amplification grow linearly, while systems with positive feedback grow non-linearly. Positive feedback loop mechanics therefore define the pathway to accelerating instability.

Loss of control in feedback systems occurs when reinforcing loops dominate system behavior, eliminating the ability to contain load growth. At this point, the system cannot maintain alignment between load and capacity because demand increases faster than capacity can respond.

This mechanism defines loss of control as the breakdown of containment. When feedback loops amplify load continuously, the system's regulatory mechanisms are overwhelmed. Load growth becomes self-sustaining and difficult to limit.

Over time, loss of control results in accelerating pressure and stress. Stable systems maintain mechanisms that limit feedback effects, preserving alignment. Unstable systems experience uncontrolled amplification, leading to rapid divergence between load and capacity.

The contrast highlights that control depends on limiting feedback. Systems that constrain amplification remain stable, while systems that allow unrestricted feedback lose the ability to maintain equilibrium. Loss of control therefore marks the transition from manageable growth to runaway escalation.

Feedback differs from drift in that it produces accelerating load growth rather than gradual baseline increase. Drift operates incrementally over time, while feedback amplifies load through recursive interaction. These mechanisms represent distinct forms of system change.

This mechanism defines drift as gradual and feedback as non-linear. Drift increases baseline at a steady rate, while feedback increases load at an accelerating rate. Feedback can incorporate drift but extends beyond it through amplification.

Over time, drift produces gradual pressure growth, while feedback produces rapid escalation. Stable systems may manage drift through alignment, but feedback challenges stability by increasing load faster than capacity can adjust.

The contrast shows that drift is predictable and continuous, while feedback is dynamic and accelerating. Systems experiencing drift alone may remain stable longer, while systems with feedback loops reach instability more quickly. Feedback therefore represents a more aggressive form of structural change.

Feedback differs from shock because it operates continuously through amplification rather than as a discrete event. Shock introduces a sudden increase in load, while feedback generates ongoing escalation through repeated cycles. These mechanisms differ in both structure and temporal behavior.

This mechanism defines shock as episodic and feedback as continuous. Shock produces immediate pressure that may dissipate, while feedback produces sustained growth that compounds over time. Feedback does not rely on a single event but on repeated amplification.

Over time, shock creates acute disruption, while feedback creates chronic escalation. Stable systems may absorb shocks without long-term impact, but feedback can gradually or rapidly exceed capacity through accumulation.

The contrast shows that shock tests system resilience at a point, while feedback reshapes system behavior over time. Feedback therefore represents a persistent source of instability, distinct from the temporary disruption caused by shock.

Compounding and acceleration occur when feedback loops cause load to increase at an increasing rate across intervals. This transition from linear to accelerating growth defines how systems move from manageable expansion to instability. Each cycle adds more load than the previous one.

This mechanism defines compounding as cumulative amplification. As load increases, it generates larger increments in subsequent cycles, creating a curve of accelerating demand. This effect distinguishes feedback-driven systems from those with proportional growth.

Over time, compounding leads to rapid divergence between load and capacity. Stable systems prevent compounding by limiting feedback effects. Unstable systems experience accelerating growth that quickly exceeds capacity, leading to pressure accumulation and stress.

The contrast shows that compounding transforms gradual change into rapid escalation. Systems without compounding remain within predictable bounds, while systems with compounding exceed those bounds. Acceleration therefore defines the speed at which instability develops under feedback conditions.

Runaway spending in expense systems operates as a feedback-driven mechanism in which load escalates beyond available capacity. This escalation is self-reinforcing, driven by internal dynamics rather than external factors. It represents the culmination of feedback loop effects.

This mechanism defines runaway spending as uncontrolled load growth. When feedback loops dominate, each cycle increases demand beyond prior levels, creating continuous pressure. The system becomes unable to maintain alignment with capacity.

Over time, runaway spending leads to rapid accumulation of stress and eventual system breakdown. Stable systems prevent runaway conditions by limiting feedback amplification. Unstable systems allow loops to persist, driving continuous escalation.

The contrast reinforces that runaway spending is not the result of isolated events but of reinforcing dynamics. Systems without feedback remain stable, while systems with uncontrolled feedback experience accelerating instability. Runaway spending therefore defines the endpoint of feedback-driven system behavior.

Expense Control Without Deprivation

Control in expense systems operates as pre-configured structural constraint that limits load before it enters the system. Restriction, by contrast, functions as reactive suppression applied after load has already emerged. This distinction separates structural design from behavioral intervention.

This mechanism defines control as upstream limitation and restriction as downstream response. Control prevents excess load from entering the system by constraining pathways and magnitude in advance. Restriction attempts to manage load after it has already entered the system, requiring repeated intervention at each instance of demand.

Over time, control reduces exposure to instability by ensuring that load remains within defined bounds automatically. Stable systems rely on control to maintain alignment between load and capacity without continuous intervention. Systems dependent on restriction must repeatedly suppress emerging load, increasing the likelihood of deviation.

The contrast shows that control eliminates the need for ongoing correction, while restriction requires continuous effort. Systems structured around control maintain stability through configuration, while systems reliant on restriction remain exposed to variability and pressure. Control versus restriction therefore defines whether stability is embedded or continually enforced.

Timing of intervention in expense systems determines whether load is constrained before generation or managed after emergence. Control operates at the pre-load stage, shaping how and whether demand enters the system. Reactive approaches operate after load appears, attempting to correct imbalance.

This mechanism defines timing as the point at which system influence is applied. Pre-load intervention limits the formation of load, while post-load intervention attempts to reduce or offset it. The earlier intervention occurs in the sequence, the more effectively load is contained.

Over time, pre-load control creates stable load patterns by preventing excess demand from forming. Systems that rely on post-load adjustment encounter repeated instances of imbalance, requiring ongoing correction. Stable systems act before load generation, while unstable systems respond after load has already disrupted alignment.

The contrast illustrates that intervention timing determines system efficiency. Pre-configured control reduces variability and pressure formation, while reactive adjustment allows instability to occur before correction. Timing of intervention therefore defines whether the system prevents or manages imbalance.

Behavioral dependence in expense systems occurs when stability relies on repeated intervention at each instance of load generation. Structural independence, by contrast, exists when system configuration maintains stability without ongoing input. This distinction defines whether the system depends on continuous action or operates autonomously.

This mechanism defines behavioral dependence as reliance on repeated decisions to maintain alignment. Structural independence eliminates this reliance by embedding constraints that regulate load automatically. System behavior becomes a function of design rather than repeated intervention.

Over time, behaviorally dependent systems experience variability in outcomes because each decision introduces potential deviation. Structurally independent systems maintain consistent performance because load generation is bounded by configuration. Stable systems minimize dependence on repeated intervention, while unstable systems require continuous adjustment.

The contrast shows that independence reduces exposure to instability. Systems that rely on structure maintain alignment consistently, while systems that depend on behavior are subject to variation. Behavioral dependence versus structural independence therefore defines the reliability of system stability.

Decision frequency functions as structural exposure to instability because each decision represents a point at which load can deviate from alignment. High decision frequency increases the number of opportunities for load to exceed capacity. This introduces variability into system behavior.

This mechanism defines decision frequency as the rate at which the system requires intervention to manage load. Each decision point creates a potential divergence from stable conditions. The more frequently decisions are required, the greater the system's exposure to misalignment.

Over time, systems with high decision frequency experience greater variability in load patterns. Stable systems reduce decision frequency through structural constraints, limiting opportunities for deviation. Unstable systems require frequent decisions, increasing the likelihood of inconsistent load generation.

The contrast highlights that decision frequency is not neutral. Systems that minimize decision points maintain consistent alignment, while systems with frequent decisions experience increased instability. Decision frequency therefore acts as a driver of variability and pressure within the system.

Decision reduction operates as a control mechanism by eliminating points at which load generation depends on repeated intervention. By removing these points, the system reduces exposure to variability and maintains consistent behavior. This transforms control from active management into embedded structure.

This mechanism defines decision reduction as the removal of decision-dependent pathways. When fewer decisions are required, the system operates within predefined constraints, limiting opportunities for load to exceed capacity. This reduces variability in load generation.

Over time, decision reduction stabilizes system behavior by ensuring that load remains within predictable bounds. Stable systems embed constraints that eliminate the need for frequent decisions. Unstable systems maintain numerous decision points, increasing exposure to deviation.

The contrast shows that reducing decisions enhances stability. Systems with minimal decision dependence maintain alignment automatically, while systems with high decision dependence experience variability. Decision reduction therefore functions as a core mechanism of structural control.

Structural constraint operates as pre-load control by limiting how much load can be generated before it enters the system. These constraints are embedded within the system's configuration, defining maximum load levels and pathways. This prevents excessive demand from forming.

This mechanism defines constraint as a boundary on load generation. By restricting magnitude and pathways, the system ensures that demand remains within capacity limits. This control occurs before load interacts with capacity, reducing the likelihood of pressure.

Over time, structural constraint maintains stable load patterns by preventing excessive variation. Stable systems enforce constraints that limit load generation consistently. Unstable systems lack such constraints, allowing load to expand beyond capacity.

The contrast highlights that constraint is preventive rather than corrective. Systems with structural constraints maintain alignment by design, while systems without them rely on reactive measures. Structural constraint therefore defines how control is embedded within the system.

Load pathway design determines how demand enters the system by defining the channels through which expenses are generated. These pathways shape load structure, influencing magnitude, timing, and variability. Proper design constrains how load flows into the system.

This mechanism defines pathway design as the configuration of entry points for load. By limiting or structuring these pathways, the system controls how demand is introduced. This reduces the potential for excessive or irregular load.

Over time, well-designed pathways produce consistent and predictable load patterns. Stable systems maintain controlled pathways that align with capacity. Unstable systems allow unrestricted pathways, increasing variability and pressure formation.

The contrast shows that pathway design influences behavior at the source of load. Systems with structured pathways maintain alignment, while systems with open pathways experience uncontrolled demand. Load pathway design therefore acts as a foundational control mechanism.

Bounded magnitude in expense systems refers to load constrained within defined limits, while open magnitude allows unrestricted expansion. This distinction determines whether the system can maintain alignment between load and capacity.

This mechanism defines bounded magnitude as capped demand and open magnitude as unbounded demand. When load is bounded, it remains within predictable limits that capacity can absorb. When load is open, it can expand beyond capacity, creating pressure.

Over time, bounded systems maintain stability by ensuring that load does not exceed capacity. Open systems experience variability and escalation as load expands without constraint. Stable systems enforce magnitude limits, while unstable systems allow unrestricted growth.

The contrast highlights that magnitude control is essential for stability. Systems with bounded load maintain alignment, while systems with open load risk imbalance. Bounded versus open magnitude therefore defines whether load remains manageable within the system.

Variability compression through structure reduces the range of load fluctuation within defined bounds without eliminating variation entirely. This is achieved by embedding constraints that limit how much load can vary across intervals. The system maintains flexibility within those bounds.

This mechanism defines variability compression as controlled fluctuation. By restricting the amplitude of variation, the system ensures that changes in load remain within capacity limits. This prevents extreme deviations that could create pressure.

Over time, compressed variability produces stable load patterns that align with capacity. Stable systems maintain bounded fluctuation, preserving continuity. Unstable systems allow wide variability, increasing the likelihood of imbalance.

The contrast shows that variability does not need to be eliminated to achieve stability. Systems with compressed variability maintain flexibility while preventing instability. Variability compression therefore defines how structure can manage fluctuation without removing it.

Reactive adjustment operates after load has been generated, attempting to correct imbalance, while structural stability prevents imbalance through pre-configured constraints. This distinction defines whether the system manages or avoids instability.

This mechanism defines reactive adjustment as post-load correction and structural stability as pre-load prevention. Reactive systems respond to imbalance after it occurs, while structural systems prevent imbalance from forming.

Over time, reactive systems experience recurring pressure events that require continuous correction. Structural systems maintain alignment without repeated intervention. Stable systems rely on pre-configured constraints, while unstable systems depend on ongoing adjustment.

The contrast highlights that prevention is more effective than correction. Systems that prevent imbalance maintain stability consistently, while systems that react to imbalance remain exposed to variability. Reactive adjustment versus structural stability therefore defines system reliability.

Behavioral dependence in expense systems arises when stability depends on repeated intervention, while structural relief occurs when configuration eliminates the need for such intervention. This distinction defines whether the system requires continuous effort to maintain alignment.

This mechanism defines behavioral dependence as the cumulative burden of repeated decision-making. Each intervention requires effort to maintain stability. Structural relief removes this burden by embedding constraints that regulate load automatically.

Over time, systems with behavioral dependence experience variability because of inconsistent intervention. Systems with structural relief maintain consistent alignment without ongoing input. Stable systems minimize strain by relying on structure, while unstable systems depend on repeated effort.

The contrast shows that effort-dependent systems are inherently less stable than configuration-based systems. Structural relief provides consistency, while behavioral dependence introduces variability. This distinction defines the efficiency of system design in maintaining stability.

Control as a stability mechanism operates through structural configuration that limits load generation and maintains alignment with capacity. It ensures that demand remains within defined bounds, preventing pressure formation and reducing variability.

This mechanism defines control as embedded system design rather than active management. By constraining pathways, magnitude, and variability, the system maintains stability without requiring continuous intervention. Control operates continuously through configuration.

Over time, controlled systems exhibit consistent load patterns and reduced exposure to instability. Stable systems rely on control to maintain alignment automatically. Unstable systems lack such configuration, resulting in variability and pressure.

The contrast reinforces that stability emerges from structure, not repeated intervention. Systems with control maintain alignment through design, while systems without control depend on ongoing correction. Control therefore defines the foundation of stable expense systems.

Structural Reduction vs Behavioral Reduction

Reduction in expense systems operates as a mechanism that decreases load within the system across time rather than as a descriptive outcome of lower spending. It must be defined by how load is altered structurally across time, not by a single observation of reduced outflow. This establishes reduction as an active system process that changes how load is generated and sustained.

This mechanism defines reduction as transformation of load pathways or magnitude within the system's configuration. A reduction is not complete when load decreases in a single interval; it is only complete when the system produces lower load consistently without additional intervention. This distinction separates temporary change from structural modification.

Across time, reduction manifests either as persistent change or as transient fluctuation. Stable systems exhibit reduction that remains embedded across intervals, maintaining lower load continuously. Unstable systems display reductions that appear briefly and then reverse, indicating no structural change.

The contrast shows that reduction must be evaluated through persistence rather than observation. Systems that structurally reduce load maintain alignment with capacity more reliably, while systems that only temporarily reduce load remain exposed to pressure. Reduction therefore functions as a mechanism that reshapes system behavior over time.

Structural reduction differs because it alters the system's configuration to permanently lower baseline load, while behavioral reduction suppresses load temporarily without changing underlying structure. This distinction defines whether reduction is embedded or requires repeated intervention.

This mechanism defines structural reduction as baseline modification and behavioral reduction as surface suppression. Structural reduction removes or reconfigures load pathways so that demand does not reappear. Behavioral reduction limits load at the point of emergence but leaves pathways intact, allowing reversion.

Across time, structural reduction produces consistent lower load without additional input. Behavioral reduction produces intermittent decreases followed by reappearance of load. Stable systems rely on structural reduction to maintain alignment, while unstable systems depend on behavioral suppression.

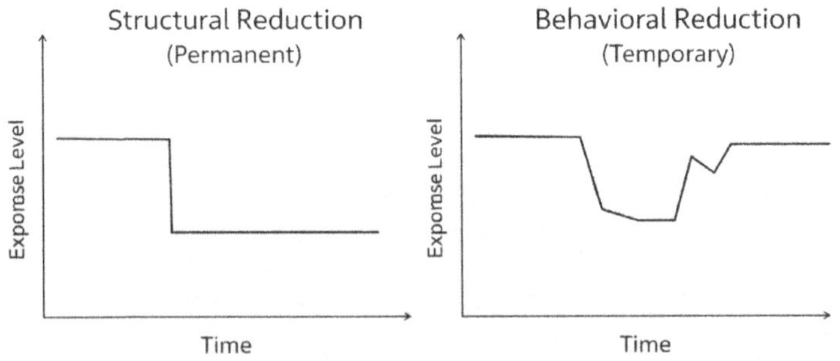

[Figure 9: Structural vs Behavioral Reduction — durable vs temporary changes]

The contrast highlights durability as the defining variable. Structural reduction persists because it changes the system, while behavioral reduction fades because it does not. This distinction determines whether reduction contributes to stability or remains temporary.

Temporary suppression in expense systems occurs when load is reduced within a limited interval but returns in subsequent periods. Permanent change occurs when reduction persists across intervals due to altered system configuration. This distinction defines the temporal behavior of reduction.

This mechanism defines suppression as short-term adjustment and permanent change as structural persistence. Suppression reduces load at the point of intervention but does not prevent its recurrence. Permanent change eliminates or modifies load pathways, ensuring that reduction continues without further input.

Across time, temporary suppression produces oscillation between lower and higher load levels. Permanent change produces a sustained shift to lower load. Stable systems achieve persistence through structural change, while unstable systems exhibit repeated suppression and reversion.

The contrast shows that duration determines effectiveness. Systems that rely on suppression experience recurring variability and pressure. Systems that achieve permanent change maintain reduced load consistently. Temporary suppression versus permanent change therefore defines whether reduction stabilizes or fluctuates.

Baseline reduction targets the system's structural floor by lowering persistent load, while surface reduction affects variable or discretionary layers without altering baseline. This distinction determines whether reduction influences the system's minimum operating requirement or only its upper layers.

This mechanism defines baseline reduction as structural change and surface reduction as superficial adjustment. When baseline is reduced, the system's minimum load decreases across all intervals. When only surface load is reduced, baseline remains unchanged, and persistent demand continues to define system pressure.

Across time, baseline reduction creates lasting improvement in alignment between load and capacity. Surface reduction produces temporary relief but does not change the system's core demand. Stable systems prioritize baseline modification, while unstable systems rely on surface adjustments.

The contrast highlights that baseline defines long-term stability. Systems with reduced baseline maintain lower pressure consistently, while systems with unchanged baseline remain constrained. Baseline versus surface reduction therefore determines whether reduction alters structural conditions or only temporary states.

Reversion dynamics in expense systems emerge when temporarily reduced load returns to prior levels due to unchanged structure. This process reflects the system's tendency to revert to its original configuration when pathways remain intact. Reversion indicates that reduction has not been embedded.

This mechanism defines reversion as the reappearance of load after suppression. When reduction depends on continuous intervention, the absence of that intervention allows load to return. This creates cyclical patterns of decrease and increase rather than sustained reduction.

Across time, reversion produces oscillating load behavior. Stable systems prevent reversion by altering structure, ensuring that reduced load does not reappear. Unstable systems experience repeated reversion, maintaining exposure to pressure and variability.

The contrast shows that reversion is a structural signal. Systems with persistent reduction do not revert because pathways have changed. Systems with temporary suppression revert because pathways remain unchanged. Reversion dynamics therefore define whether reduction is durable or transient.

Durability functions as the primary variable in evaluating reduction because it determines whether lower load persists across time. Reduction that endures across intervals alters system behavior, while reduction that does not endure has limited structural impact. Durability defines effectiveness.

This mechanism defines durability as persistence without intervention. A durable reduction remains in place automatically, requiring no repeated input to maintain lower load. Non-durable reduction depends on ongoing intervention and is therefore subject to variability.

Across time, durable reduction produces consistent alignment between load and capacity. Non-durable reduction produces intermittent alignment followed by reversion. Stable systems achieve durability through structural change, while unstable systems rely on temporary suppression.

The contrast highlights that persistence outweighs magnitude. A smaller but durable reduction has greater long-term impact than a larger but temporary one. Durability therefore determines whether reduction contributes to stability or remains inconsequential.

Structural reduction operates as baseline reconfiguration by lowering the system's minimum operating load. This change alters the persistent demand that exists in every interval, redefining the system's structural floor. It represents a fundamental shift in how load is generated.

This mechanism defines reconfiguration as modification of baseline conditions. By removing or altering persistent load, the system reduces its continuous demand on capacity. This change affects all future intervals, not just isolated instances.

Across time, baseline reconfiguration produces sustained reduction in pressure and increased operating margin. Stable systems maintain reduced baseline through structural change. Unstable systems retain high baseline, limiting the impact of temporary reductions.

The contrast shows that baseline reconfiguration has system-wide effects. Systems with lower baseline experience improved stability across all intervals, while systems without reconfiguration remain constrained. Structural reduction therefore functions as a foundational mechanism for stability.

Behavioral reduction introduces variability because suppression of load is inconsistent across intervals. Without structural change, load reappears irregularly, creating fluctuations in demand. This variability increases exposure to pressure and instability.

This mechanism defines behavioral reduction as intermittent suppression. Each instance of reduced load depends on intervention, and absence of intervention allows load to return. This creates uneven patterns of load across time.

Across time, variability reintroduced through behavioral reduction disrupts alignment between load and capacity. Stable systems minimize variability by embedding reduction structurally. Unstable systems experience fluctuating load due to inconsistent suppression.

The contrast highlights that behavioral reduction increases instability despite temporary decreases in load. Systems that rely on suppression experience irregular patterns, while systems with structural reduction maintain consistency. Behavioral reduction therefore contributes to variability rather than stability.

Decision dependence in behavioral reduction occurs when maintaining lower load requires repeated intervention at each instance of demand. This dependence introduces variability because each decision point represents a potential deviation from reduction.

This mechanism defines decision dependence as reliance on continuous input. When reduction is not embedded structurally, each interval requires action to maintain lower load. This creates exposure to inconsistency and variability.

Across time, systems with high decision dependence exhibit fluctuating load patterns. Stable systems reduce or eliminate decision dependence through structural change. Unstable systems maintain numerous decision points, increasing instability.

The contrast shows that decision dependence undermines persistence. Systems that require repeated intervention cannot maintain consistent reduction, while systems that eliminate decision dependence achieve stability. Decision dependence therefore acts as a driver of reversion and variability.

Reduction differs from drift in that it decreases baseline load, while drift increases it gradually over time. These mechanisms operate in opposite directions, shaping the system's long-term trajectory. Reduction lowers persistent demand, while drift raises it.

This mechanism defines reduction as structural contraction and drift as structural expansion. Reduction moves baseline downward, increasing margin and reducing pressure. Drift moves baseline upward, compressing margin and increasing pressure.

Across time, reduction counteracts the effects of drift by reversing baseline expansion. Stable systems maintain reduction to preserve alignment, while unstable systems experience drift that increases load and reduces stability.

The contrast highlights opposing dynamics. Systems dominated by reduction improve stability over time, while systems dominated by drift move toward instability. Reduction versus drift therefore defines the direction of system change.

Magnitude versus persistence tradeoff defines the difference between large temporary reductions and smaller durable reductions. This tradeoff determines whether reduction produces immediate impact or long-term stability. Persistence ultimately governs system behavior.

This mechanism defines magnitude as the size of reduction and persistence as its duration. Large reductions that are not sustained have limited structural impact. Smaller reductions that persist across intervals reshape system behavior more effectively.

Across time, persistent reductions accumulate, producing greater overall impact than temporary large changes. Stable systems prioritize persistence through structural change. Unstable systems focus on magnitude without durability, leading to reversion.

The contrast shows that persistence outweighs scale. Systems with durable reduction maintain alignment consistently, while systems with large but temporary reduction experience recurring instability. Magnitude versus persistence therefore defines effectiveness of reduction.

Structural reduction as a stability mechanism operates by permanently lowering baseline load, reducing pressure and variability across the system. It ensures that load remains within capacity without requiring repeated intervention. This establishes reduction as a foundational driver of stability.

This mechanism defines structural reduction as configuration-based control of load. By altering pathways and baseline, the system maintains lower demand automatically. This reduces exposure to pressure and stress.

Across time, structural reduction produces consistent alignment and increased operating margin. Stable systems rely on this mechanism to maintain low baseline and predictable load patterns. Unstable systems lack structural reduction, remaining exposed to drift and variability.

The contrast reinforces that stability emerges from persistent configuration. Systems with structural reduction maintain alignment without intervention, while systems without it depend on temporary suppression. Structural reduction therefore defines how durable change leads to sustained system stability.

Expense Smoothing

Variability in expense systems operates as uneven load distribution across time, where demand is applied irregularly rather than consistently. This defines variability not simply as fluctuation in magnitude, but as inconsistency in how load is sequenced across intervals. Uneven distribution creates conditions where some intervals carry disproportionately higher demand.

This mechanism defines irregular load as misaligned temporal distribution. When load is clustered into certain intervals, those intervals experience elevated demand relative to capacity. Other intervals may remain underutilized, creating imbalance in how the system absorbs load over time.

Across time, uneven distribution produces instability by concentrating demand into specific points. Stable systems maintain more uniform distribution, ensuring that load remains aligned with capacity in each interval. Unstable systems exhibit irregular patterns that generate localized imbalance.

The contrast shows that distribution matters independently of total load. Systems with identical totals can experience different stability outcomes based on how load is distributed. Variability as uneven distribution therefore defines a primary structural source of pressure.

Clustering in expense systems emerges when multiple load elements converge within the same interval, concentrating demand into a narrow time frame. This concentration increases the intensity of load-capacity interaction at specific points, creating elevated risk of imbalance.

This mechanism defines clustering as temporal aggregation of load. Instead of being spread across intervals, multiple demands are applied simultaneously or in close sequence. This aggregation amplifies the load within that interval, increasing its impact on capacity.

Across time, clustering produces repeated instances of concentrated demand. Stable systems distribute load to prevent convergence, maintaining consistent interaction with capacity. Unstable systems allow clustering to persist, creating periodic spikes.

The contrast highlights that clustering transforms moderate load into high-intensity events. Systems without clustering maintain balanced distribution, while systems with clustering experience concentrated pressure. Clustering therefore acts as a precursor to spike formation and instability.

Spike formation in expense systems occurs when clustered load exceeds the system's absorptive capacity within a single interval. These spikes represent localized peaks in demand that surpass what capacity can handle at that moment. Spike formation is the direct result of concentrated load.

This mechanism defines spikes as elevated load peaks generated by uneven distribution. When multiple demands converge, their combined magnitude creates a peak that differs significantly from surrounding intervals. This peak creates immediate imbalance.

Across time, spike formation introduces episodic instability into the system. Stable systems minimize spike formation by distributing load evenly. Unstable systems experience recurring spikes due to persistent clustering.

The contrast shows that spikes are not inherent to total load but to its distribution. Systems with evenly distributed load avoid spikes, while systems with concentrated load experience them regularly. Spike formation therefore represents the transition from variability to pressure.

Pressure in expense systems emerges when concentrated load within an interval exceeds available capacity. This imbalance occurs at the point of spike formation, where demand surpasses absorptive ability. Concentrated load compresses the system's margin, creating immediate pressure.

This mechanism defines pressure as the outcome of peak demand exceeding capacity. Unlike distributed load, which may be absorbed gradually, concentrated load requires immediate capacity. When capacity is insufficient, pressure forms instantly.

Across time, repeated pressure events arise from recurring concentration patterns. Stable systems maintain distribution that prevents concentrated demand from exceeding capacity. Unstable systems experience frequent pressure due to recurring spikes.

The contrast illustrates that pressure is driven by distribution as much as magnitude. Systems with balanced distribution maintain alignment, while systems with concentrated load experience imbalance. Pressure from concentrated load therefore defines the direct impact of uneven distribution.

Repeated stress in expense systems develops when irregular load patterns produce recurring pressure across intervals. Each instance of concentrated demand contributes to accumulated stress, creating layered stress over time. Irregular patterns prevent the system from stabilizing.

This mechanism defines stress as the accumulation of pressure events caused by uneven distribution. When spikes occur repeatedly, the system does not fully recover between intervals. This leads to sustained stress.

Across time, irregular patterns amplify instability by increasing the frequency of pressure. Stable systems maintain consistent patterns that allow recovery and prevent accumulation. Unstable systems exhibit irregular distribution that produces continuous stress.

The contrast shows that consistency determines recovery. Systems with stable patterns absorb load without accumulating stress, while systems with irregular patterns experience layered pressure. Repeated stress therefore reflects the long-term impact of uneven distribution.

Temporal redistribution in expense systems operates as the reallocation of load across intervals to achieve more even distribution. This mechanism shifts demand away from concentrated points, spreading it across time to align with capacity. Redistribution changes how load interacts with capacity without altering total magnitude.

This mechanism defines redistribution as structural adjustment of timing. By reallocating when load is applied, the system reduces concentration and lowers peak demand. This improves alignment between load and capacity in each interval.

Across time, redistribution produces more consistent load patterns. Stable systems apply redistribution to maintain even demand. Unstable systems retain concentrated patterns, leading to spikes and pressure.

The contrast highlights that redistribution affects timing, not magnitude. Systems with redistributed load maintain stability through balanced interaction, while systems without redistribution experience uneven demand. Temporal redistribution therefore defines how smoothing begins.

Smoothing in expense systems functions as structural redistribution that converts irregular load into consistent, repeatable patterns. It operates by embedding redistribution into the system's configuration, ensuring that load is applied evenly across intervals. This creates stable interaction with capacity.

This mechanism defines smoothing as pattern transformation. Instead of responding to spikes, smoothing reshapes load distribution to prevent them. This establishes a consistent pattern of demand that aligns with capacity.

Across time, smoothing produces predictable load behavior. Stable systems maintain smoothed distribution, preserving alignment and reducing variability. Unstable systems retain irregular patterns, resulting in repeated spikes.

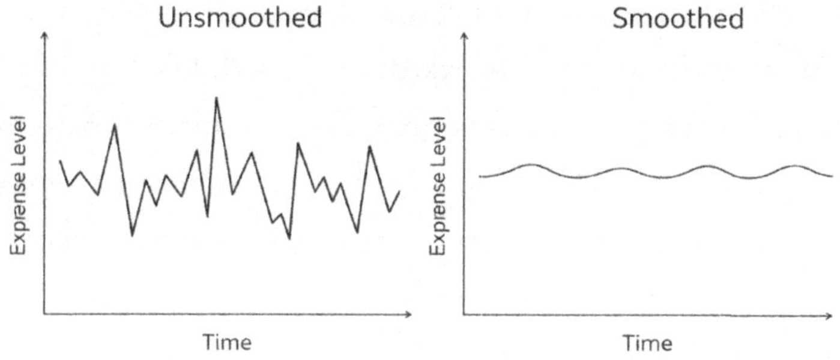

[Figure 10: Expense Smoothing — spikes flattened into stable pattern]

The contrast shows that smoothing is structural rather than reactive. Systems that smooth load maintain continuous stability, while systems that do not experience episodic disruption. Smoothing therefore defines how distribution becomes a stability mechanism.

Spike compression in expense systems operates by flattening peaks in load distribution, reducing the magnitude of demand within any single interval. This is achieved through redistribution that spreads load across multiple intervals, lowering peak intensity.

This mechanism defines compression as reduction of peak amplitude without reducing total load. By distributing demand more evenly, the system prevents extreme spikes that exceed capacity. This maintains load within absorptive limits.

Across time, spike compression reduces the frequency and severity of pressure events. Stable systems maintain compressed load patterns that align with capacity. Unstable systems experience uncompressed spikes, leading to repeated imbalance.

The contrast highlights that compression transforms load behavior. Systems with compressed spikes maintain stability, while systems with uncompressed spikes experience pressure. Spike compression therefore defines how smoothing reduces peak-driven instability.

Predictability in expense systems emerges as a result of consistent load distribution across intervals. When load patterns become repeatable, the system can anticipate demand and align capacity accordingly. Predictability is not imposed but arises from structured distribution.

This mechanism defines predictability as the outcome of smoothing. Consistent patterns reduce uncertainty in load application, allowing the system to maintain alignment. Irregular patterns, by contrast, reduce predictability and increase instability.

Across time, predictable systems exhibit stable interaction between load and capacity. Stable systems maintain consistent patterns, enabling accurate anticipation of demand. Unstable systems experience irregular patterns that disrupt forecasting.

The contrast shows that predictability is a consequence of structure. Systems with smoothed distribution achieve consistent behavior, while systems with irregular distribution remain unpredictable. Predictability therefore reflects the success of smoothing as a structural mechanism.

Alignment with capacity in expense systems occurs when load distribution matches the system's ability to absorb demand across intervals. Smoothing facilitates this alignment by ensuring that load remains within capacity at each point in time.

This mechanism defines alignment as synchronization between distributed load and available capacity. When load is evenly distributed, capacity can absorb demand consistently. When load is uneven, capacity is exceeded during spikes.

Across time, aligned systems maintain continuous stability without pressure. Stable systems ensure that distributed load does not exceed capacity in any interval. Unstable systems experience misalignment due to uneven distribution.

The contrast highlights that alignment depends on distribution. Systems with smoothed load maintain synchronization, while systems with irregular load experience imbalance. Alignment with capacity therefore defines the operational outcome of smoothing.

Continuity stabilization in expense systems occurs when smoothing eliminates episodic disruption, creating uninterrupted alignment between load and capacity. This transforms the system from one characterized by spikes to one defined by consistent operation.

This mechanism defines continuity as sustained alignment across intervals. By removing spikes and irregular patterns, the system avoids interruptions caused by pressure events. This produces stable, ongoing interaction between load and capacity.

Across time, continuity stabilization reduces stress by preventing repeated pressure events. Stable systems maintain continuous operation through smoothed distribution. Unstable systems experience episodic disruption due to uneven load.

The contrast shows that continuity is achieved through consistency. Systems with stable patterns maintain uninterrupted operation, while systems with irregular patterns experience repeated breakdowns. Continuity stabilization therefore defines the long-term effect of smoothing.

Smoothing as a stability mechanism operates by transforming uneven load distribution into consistent patterns that align with capacity. It reduces variability, compresses spikes, and creates predictable load behavior across time. This establishes smoothing as a structural driver of stability.

This mechanism defines smoothing as redistribution-based control of load. By altering how demand is applied, the system prevents concentration and reduces pressure. This maintains alignment without requiring reduction in total load.

Across time, smoothing produces sustained stability by eliminating irregular patterns and ensuring consistent interaction with capacity. Stable systems rely on smoothing to maintain continuity. Unstable systems retain uneven distribution, leading to recurring instability.

The contrast reinforces that stability depends on distribution, not just magnitude. Systems with smoothed load maintain alignment, while systems with uneven load experience pressure and stress. Smoothing therefore defines how temporal distribution governs system stability.

Constraint Design

Constraints in expense systems operate as structural limits on load that define the boundaries within which load can be generated. These limits are embedded in the system's configuration and determine the maximum allowable forms of load before it enters the system. This establishes constraints as pre-configured conditions rather than reactive responses.

This mechanism defines constraints as boundary conditions that shape load behavior at the point of origin. By limiting the range of possible load outcomes, constraints prevent excessive demand from forming. This differs from mechanisms that act after load is already present.

Across time, constrained systems maintain consistent alignment between load and capacity because demand is inherently bounded. Unconstrained systems allow load to expand freely, increasing exposure to pressure and instability. The presence or absence of constraints defines how load behaves before interaction with capacity.

The contrast shows that constraints operate upstream of load formation. Systems with embedded limits maintain stability through prevention, while systems without constraints rely on downstream correction. Constraints therefore define the structural boundaries that govern system behavior.

Constraint differs structurally from restriction because it embeds limits within the system, while restriction suppresses load after it appears. Constraints operate as pre-load boundaries, whereas restriction functions as post-load intervention. This distinction defines whether limits are structural or reactive.

This mechanism defines constraint as inherent limitation and restriction as applied suppression. When constraints are present, load cannot exceed predefined boundaries. When restriction is used, load must first emerge before it can be reduced, requiring repeated intervention.

Across time, constrained systems maintain stable load patterns without continuous adjustment. Systems dependent on restriction experience recurring demand that must be repeatedly suppressed. Stable systems rely on constraint to prevent excess load, while unstable systems depend on restriction to manage it.

The contrast highlights that constraint eliminates the need for repeated action, while restriction depends on it. Systems with constraints remain within capacity limits, while systems using restriction remain exposed to variability. Constraint versus restriction therefore defines whether stability is embedded or enforced.

Constraint differs from control in that it defines the boundaries of allowable load, while control shapes how load pathways operate within those boundaries. Constraint establishes limits, while control organizes the flow of demand through the system. These mechanisms operate at different levels.

This mechanism defines constraint as boundary definition and control as pathway shaping. Constraints determine what is possible within the system, while control determines how demand moves within those possibilities. Together, they influence load behavior but remain distinct.

Across time, systems with constraints but without effective control may still experience uneven load distribution within limits. Systems with control but without constraints may organize load but allow it to exceed capacity. Stable systems integrate both mechanisms to maintain alignment.

The contrast shows that constraint sets the outer limits, while control manages internal dynamics. Systems lacking constraint allow unrestricted expansion, while systems lacking control experience disorganized flow. Constraint versus control therefore defines the relationship between boundaries and pathways.

Boundary conditions in expense systems define the allowable range of load that the system can generate and sustain. These conditions establish upper and lower limits on demand, shaping how load behaves across all intervals. They function as the system's structural constraints.

This mechanism defines boundary conditions as fixed parameters within which load must operate. By setting these limits, the system prevents load from exceeding capacity. These boundaries apply consistently across time, ensuring that demand remains within defined ranges.

Across time, boundary conditions create predictable load behavior. Stable systems operate within these limits, maintaining alignment with capacity. Unstable systems lack clear boundaries, allowing load to exceed sustainable levels.

The contrast highlights that boundary conditions determine system stability. Systems with defined limits maintain consistent behavior, while systems without limits experience variability and pressure. Boundary conditions therefore define the permissible space in which load operates.

Pre-load regulation functions in expense systems as the limitation of demand before it is generated. This mechanism ensures that load entering the system is already constrained by structural boundaries. It prevents excessive demand from forming rather than correcting it after emergence.

This mechanism defines regulation as upstream limitation. By acting before load interacts with capacity, pre-load regulation reduces the likelihood of imbalance. It shapes the system's inputs rather than its responses.

Across time, pre-load regulation produces stable load patterns that remain within capacity limits. Stable systems rely on this mechanism to maintain alignment consistently. Unstable systems lack pre-load regulation, resulting in recurring pressure and the need for reactive adjustment.

The contrast shows that regulation is more effective than correction. Systems that regulate load before generation maintain stability, while systems that adjust after generation remain exposed to imbalance. Pre-load regulation therefore defines proactive stability within the system.

Open load systems operate without structural constraints, allowing load to enter through unrestricted pathways. Closed load systems, by contrast, define structural boundaries that limit how and when load can be generated. This distinction determines whether the system is exposed to uncontrolled demand.

This mechanism defines open systems as unbounded and closed systems as constrained. In open systems, load pathways allow unrestricted expansion, increasing variability and pressure. In closed systems, pathways are limited, ensuring that load remains within capacity.

Across time, open systems experience fluctuating and potentially escalating load patterns. Closed systems maintain consistent and predictable demand. Stable systems operate as closed systems with defined constraints, while unstable systems resemble open systems.

The contrast highlights that openness increases exposure to instability. Systems without boundaries allow load to exceed capacity, while systems with boundaries maintain alignment. Open versus closed load systems therefore defines the degree of control over demand.

Magnitude constraints in expense systems operate as limits on the maximum level of load that can be generated within any interval. These constraints cap demand, ensuring that load does not exceed capacity. This mechanism directly limits the size of potential imbalance.

This mechanism defines magnitude constraints as upper boundaries on load. By capping demand, the system prevents extreme spikes that could create pressure. This keeps load within manageable levels.

Across time, magnitude constraints produce stable load patterns by limiting peak demand. Stable systems enforce these constraints consistently, maintaining alignment with capacity. Unstable systems lack such limits, allowing load to expand beyond capacity.

The contrast shows that limiting magnitude reduces instability. Systems with capped load avoid extreme pressure events, while systems without constraints experience spikes. Magnitude constraints therefore define how peak demand is controlled within the system.

Pathway constraints in expense systems operate by limiting the channels through which load can enter the system. These constraints define which pathways are available and how they function, shaping the structure of demand generation.

This mechanism defines pathway constraints as restrictions on entry points for load. By controlling these pathways, the system reduces the likelihood of excessive or irregular demand. This influences both magnitude and distribution of load.

Across time, constrained pathways produce consistent and predictable load patterns. Stable systems maintain limited and structured pathways, ensuring alignment with capacity. Unstable systems allow unrestricted pathways, increasing variability and pressure.

The contrast highlights that pathway design determines how load is introduced. Systems with constrained pathways maintain stability, while systems with open pathways experience uncontrolled demand. Pathway constraints therefore define how load enters the system.

Constraint stability in expense systems arises from pre-configured boundaries that prevent imbalance, while reactive adjustment responds to imbalance after it occurs. This distinction defines whether stability is maintained proactively or restored after disruption.

This mechanism defines constraint stability as prevention and reactive adjustment as correction. Systems with constraints avoid excessive load, maintaining alignment continuously. Systems relying on adjustment experience imbalance and must correct it repeatedly.

Across time, constraint-based systems maintain consistent stability without recurring pressure. Reactive systems experience cycles of imbalance and correction. Stable systems rely on constraints to prevent instability, while unstable systems depend on adjustment to manage it.

The contrast shows that prevention is more efficient than correction. Systems with constraint stability remain aligned, while systems relying on adjustment remain exposed to variability. Constraint stability versus reactive adjustment therefore defines the mode of system operation.

Constraint interaction with variability in expense systems operates by bounding the range of load fluctuation. Constraints limit how much load can vary across intervals, reducing the amplitude of variability without eliminating it entirely.

This mechanism defines bounded variability as controlled fluctuation within predefined limits. By constraining variation, the system ensures that load remains within capacity even when it changes. This reduces the likelihood of pressure.

Across time, constrained variability produces stable load patterns with predictable ranges. Stable systems maintain variability within bounds, preserving alignment. Unstable systems allow wide fluctuations, increasing instability.

The contrast highlights that variability is not inherently destabilizing if bounded. Systems with constraints maintain manageable fluctuation, while systems without constraints experience extreme variation. Constraint interaction with variability therefore defines how fluctuation is controlled.

Constraint interaction with drift in expense systems operates by limiting the upward expansion of baseline load over time. Constraints act as caps that prevent baseline from increasing beyond defined limits. This counteracts the gradual expansion associated with drift.

This mechanism defines drift limitation as structural resistance to baseline increase. By setting boundaries on load growth, the system prevents incremental expansion from accumulating. This preserves margin and stability.

Across time, constrained systems resist drift by maintaining baseline within limits. Stable systems prevent baseline expansion through embedded constraints. Unstable systems allow drift to proceed unchecked, leading to margin compression.

The contrast shows that constraints define the trajectory of baseline. Systems with limits maintain a consistent baseline, while systems without limits experience expansion. Constraint interaction with drift therefore determines long-term system stability.

Constraint design in expense systems operates as a proactive stability mechanism by embedding boundaries that limit load before it is generated. These boundaries prevent excessive demand, ensuring that load remains aligned with capacity across all intervals.

This mechanism defines constraint design as intentional configuration of limits. By shaping the system's allowable load, it prevents pressure and reduces variability. This creates consistent and predictable system behavior.

Across time, constraint design produces sustained stability by maintaining bounded load patterns. Stable systems rely on constraints to preserve alignment automatically. Unstable systems lack such design, resulting in variability and pressure.

The contrast reinforces that stability emerges from defined limits. Systems with constraint design maintain alignment without intervention, while systems without it depend on reactive adjustment. Constraint design therefore defines how structural boundaries prevent system overload.

Expense Floors and Stability Margins

Expense floor is defined as the minimum load required for the system to sustain continuous operation. It represents the lowest level of load that cannot be removed without altering the system's configuration. This establishes the floor as a structural threshold rather than a fluctuating value.

Expense floor corresponds to baseline load as the system's minimum persistent requirement.

This mechanism defines the floor as distinct from general load because it persists across all intervals regardless of variability. While total expenses may rise and fall, the expense floor remains constant unless structural changes occur. It forms the base layer of load that capacity must continuously meet.

Across time, the expense floor defines the system's minimum required capacity. Stable systems maintain sufficient capacity above this level, preserving a gap for absorption of additional load. Fragile systems operate with capacity close to the floor, leaving little tolerance for fluctuation.

The contrast shows that the expense floor is not optional or adjustable within normal operation. Systems with a well-defined floor and sufficient separation from capacity maintain stability, while systems operating at or near the floor experience immediate sensitivity to change. The expense floor therefore defines the system's minimum operating requirement.

Floor versus total expenses distinguishes persistent minimum load from the full range of load applied across time. Total expenses include both the floor and variable components, while the floor represents only the non-eliminable portion of load. This distinction separates structural requirement from fluctuating load.

This mechanism defines total expenses as composite load and the floor as foundational load. Variable and discretionary components may change across intervals, but the floor remains constant unless the system is reconfigured. This makes the floor the baseline requirement for continuous operation.

Across time, systems with identical total expenses can exhibit different stability depending on the proportion represented by the floor. Stable systems maintain a lower floor relative to capacity, preserving margin. Fragile systems have a higher floor, reducing the space available for variability.

The contrast highlights that total magnitude does not determine stability. Systems with moderate totals but high floors may be unstable, while systems with higher totals but lower floors may remain stable. Floor versus total expenses therefore defines how much of the system's load is structurally fixed.

The structural nature of the expense floor means that it is determined by system configuration rather than temporary adjustments. The floor reflects embedded requirements that persist until the structure itself is altered. This distinguishes it from load that can fluctuate without structural change.

This mechanism defines the floor as configuration-based load. It is created by persistent elements within the system that require continuous support from capacity. Changes to the floor require modification of these structural elements rather than adjustments within intervals.

Across time, the structural nature of the floor ensures its persistence. Stable systems maintain awareness of this fixed requirement and align capacity accordingly. Fragile systems underestimate the rigidity of the floor, leading to insufficient margin.

The contrast shows that the floor cannot be reduced through temporary suppression of load. Systems that treat the floor as flexible experience reversion, while systems that recognize its structural nature maintain alignment. The structural nature of the expense floor therefore defines its persistence across time.

Operating at the floor occurs when system capacity is equal to or only marginally above the expense floor, leaving minimal or no margin. In this condition, the system functions without buffer, meaning any additional load creates immediate imbalance. This defines a state of maximum sensitivity.

This mechanism defines floor-level operation as zero-margin alignment. The system is technically balanced but lacks the capacity to absorb variability or sequencing differences. This creates a condition in which stability exists only in the absence of disturbance.

Across time, operating at the floor results in frequent pressure events because even small deviations exceed capacity. Stable systems avoid this condition by maintaining distance from the floor. Fragile systems operate at or near the floor, experiencing repeated imbalance.

The contrast highlights that equilibrium at the floor is not stability but conditional balance. Systems with margin maintain resilience, while systems at the floor are exposed to immediate disruption. Operating at the floor therefore defines a high-risk system state.

Operating margin represents the distance between total available capacity and the expense floor. It defines how much additional load the system can absorb before pressure occurs. This establishes margin as a measure of system tolerance.

This mechanism defines margin as the buffer between persistent load and available resources. It is not a component of capacity itself but a relational distance that determines how much variability can be absorbed. Margin exists only when capacity exceeds the floor.

Across time, operating margin determines the system's ability to remain aligned under changing conditions. Stable systems maintain sufficient margin to absorb variability and sequencing gaps. Fragile systems have minimal margin, increasing sensitivity to deviation.

The contrast shows that margin is distinct from capacity. Systems with high capacity but high floors may have little margin, while systems with moderate capacity and low floors may have significant margin. Operating margin therefore defines the system's absorptive capacity relative to its minimum load.

Margin as an absorptive buffer functions by allowing the system to absorb variability, timing mismatch, and temporary load increases without generating pressure. It acts as a protective layer between load and capacity, maintaining alignment during fluctuations.

This mechanism defines the buffer as the space within which load can vary without exceeding capacity. When variability occurs, margin absorbs the difference, preventing imbalance. This reduces the frequency of pressure events.

Across time, systems with sufficient margin maintain stability even under irregular conditions. Stable systems use margin to absorb fluctuations and sequencing differences. Fragile systems lack sufficient margin, causing variability to convert directly into pressure.

The contrast highlights that margin transforms variability into manageable deviation. Systems without margin experience immediate imbalance, while systems with margin maintain continuity. Margin as an absorptive buffer therefore defines how systems tolerate change.

Margin versus capacity distinguishes total available resources from the usable buffer between capacity and the expense floor. Capacity represents the total inflow and liquidity available, while margin represents the portion of that capacity not required for baseline operation.

This mechanism defines margin as derived from capacity but not equivalent to it. A system may have high capacity, but if the floor is equally high, margin remains minimal. Conversely, lower-capacity systems may have significant margin if the floor is low.

Across time, systems that focus on capacity alone may overlook margin constraints. Stable systems evaluate the relationship between capacity and floor, ensuring sufficient margin. Fragile systems rely on total capacity without accounting for baseline requirements.

The contrast shows that capacity does not guarantee stability. Systems with high capacity but low margin remain sensitive to variation, while systems with moderate capacity and high margin maintain resilience. Margin versus capacity therefore defines effective system tolerance.

Low-margin system behavior is characterized by compression, sensitivity, and constrained operation due to limited distance between capacity and the expense floor. In this state, the system has little tolerance for variation or disruption.

This mechanism defines low-margin conditions as high-risk configurations. Because margin is minimal, any increase in load or delay in capacity creates immediate pressure. The system operates under continuous proximity to imbalance.

Across time, low-margin systems experience frequent pressure events and limited recovery. Stable systems maintain sufficient margin to avoid this condition. Fragile systems operate with compressed margins, leading to persistent instability.

The contrast highlights that margin determines operational flexibility. Systems with sufficient margin absorb fluctuations, while low-margin systems react to every deviation. Low-margin behavior therefore defines constrained and sensitive system operation.

Fragility emerges when minimal margin causes small deviations to generate immediate pressure. In this condition, the system lacks the capacity to absorb even minor variability or timing differences. This defines fragility as sensitivity to change.

This mechanism defines fragility as a function of insufficient buffer. When margin is low, the threshold for imbalance is minimal, meaning ordinary fluctuations exceed capacity. This creates frequent pressure events.

Across time, fragile systems accumulate stress due to repeated imbalance. Stable systems maintain margin to prevent small deviations from triggering pressure. Fragile systems operate near the floor, where minor changes produce significant effects.

The contrast shows that fragility is not determined by total load but by available margin. Systems with sufficient buffer remain stable under variation, while systems without buffer become unstable quickly. Fragility under minimal margin therefore defines sensitivity to deviation.

Margin and variability absorption are directly linked because margin determines whether fluctuations in load produce pressure. When margin is sufficient, variability remains within absorptive limits. When margin is insufficient, variability converts into imbalance.

This mechanism defines absorption as the ability to accommodate fluctuation without exceeding capacity. Margin provides the space necessary for this accommodation. Without margin, variability leads directly to pressure.

Across time, systems with adequate margin maintain stable operation despite changing load patterns. Stable systems use margin to absorb variability consistently. Fragile systems lack this capacity, resulting in repeated pressure events.

The contrast highlights that variability is not inherently destabilizing. Systems with margin can tolerate fluctuation, while systems without margin cannot. Margin and variability absorption therefore define how systems respond to change.

Margin versus timing mismatch defines the role of buffer in bridging sequence gaps between load and capacity. When load occurs before capacity, margin provides the resources necessary to maintain continuity until capacity becomes available.

This mechanism defines margin as a bridging resource in sequencing gaps. Timing mismatch creates intervals where load exceeds immediate capacity, and margin absorbs this difference. Without margin, these gaps result in pressure.

Across time, systems with sufficient margin manage timing mismatch without instability. Stable systems maintain buffer to bridge sequencing differences. Fragile systems experience immediate imbalance when timing is misaligned.

The contrast shows that timing mismatch becomes destabilizing only when margin is insufficient. Systems with margin maintain continuity, while systems without it experience pressure. Margin versus timing mismatch therefore defines the system's ability to handle sequencing gaps.

Margin versus shock defines how the system responds to sudden increases in load. When a shock occurs, margin determines whether the system can absorb the spike without generating sustained pressure. It acts as the first line of defense against abrupt load.

This mechanism defines margin as shock-absorbing capacity. When load increases suddenly, margin provides the space needed to absorb the increase without exceeding capacity. Without margin, shock creates immediate imbalance.

Across time, systems with sufficient margin contain shocks and recover quickly. Stable systems absorb shocks within their buffer, preventing long-term effects. Fragile systems experience prolonged pressure due to lack of margin.

The contrast highlights that shock impact depends on available buffer. Systems with margin maintain stability under sudden load, while systems without margin experience immediate disruption. Margin versus shock therefore defines resilience to discrete events.

Margin erosion occurs when structural changes such as drift and feedback reduce the distance between capacity and the expense floor over time. This process gradually compresses the buffer available for absorbing variability.

This mechanism defines erosion as the reduction of margin through increasing load or decreasing capacity. Drift raises the floor incrementally, while feedback can accelerate load growth, both reducing margin. This compression increases system sensitivity.

Across time, margin erosion leads to increasing fragility and more frequent pressure events. Stable systems maintain or expand margin, preserving stability. Unstable systems allow erosion to proceed, reducing tolerance to variability.

The contrast shows that margin is not static. Systems that protect margin maintain resilience, while systems that lose margin become unstable. Margin erosion therefore defines the transition from stable to fragile system states.

Floor proximity determines system sensitivity by defining how close capacity is to the expense floor. The closer the system operates to the floor, the less margin exists to absorb variation. This increases responsiveness to even minor changes.

This mechanism defines sensitivity as a function of proximity. Systems operating near the floor experience immediate effects from small deviations. Systems with greater distance maintain stability under similar conditions.

Across time, close proximity leads to frequent pressure and limited recovery. Stable systems maintain distance from the floor, reducing sensitivity. Fragile systems operate near the floor, amplifying the impact of variability.

The contrast highlights that proximity governs system response. Systems far from the floor absorb changes easily, while systems near the floor react sharply. Floor proximity therefore defines how responsive the system is to deviation.

Operating margin as a structural requirement defines margin not as optional excess but as a necessary component of system stability. Without sufficient margin, the system cannot absorb variability, timing mismatch, or shocks.

This mechanism defines margin as essential to maintaining alignment between load and capacity. It is not surplus but required buffer that ensures continuous operation under changing conditions. Systems without margin operate in a fragile state.

Across time, systems with structural margin maintain resilience and stability. Stable systems preserve margin through configuration, ensuring consistent absorption capacity. Fragile systems lack margin, leading to repeated pressure and stress.

The contrast reinforces that margin determines whether a system can sustain operation under variability. Systems with margin remain stable, while systems without margin experience instability. Operating margin therefore defines the fundamental requirement for resilient system behavior.

Expenses and Liquidity

Liquidity is defined as immediately available capacity that can absorb load at the moment expenses are applied. It is the stored portion of capacity, distinct from incoming flow, because it exists as an accessible resource before new income arrives. This establishes liquidity as a present-tense system property rather than a future expectation. In structural terms, liquidity determines whether the system can meet current load without delay. It represents the immediately accessible portion of total capacity.

This mechanism defines liquidity as usable absorptive capacity rather than nominal financial value. Resources that cannot be accessed in the interval of demand do not function as liquidity within the expense system. What matters is not nominal asset presence but immediate availability at the point of load application. Liquidity therefore operates as the system's first-line resource for maintaining continuity under active demand.

Across time, liquidity allows the system to absorb load when inflow and outflow are not perfectly synchronized. Stable systems maintain enough immediately available capacity to prevent ordinary expense application from becoming a pressure event. Depleted systems, by contrast, face each interval with reduced ability to absorb even routine load. The distinction is structural: one system possesses present absorptive capacity, while the other depends on resources that are delayed, conditional, or absent.

The contrast shows why liquidity cannot be treated as a secondary support layer. Systems with sufficient liquidity remain operational through ordinary variability and temporary imbalance, while systems without it experience immediate instability when load arrives. Liquidity therefore defines the system's accessible short-term capacity.

Liquidity differs from income because liquidity is stored capacity while income is incoming flow. Income replenishes the system over time, but liquidity determines what the system can absorb before or between inflow events. This distinction is necessary because an expense system does not operate on promised capacity alone. It operates on what is available when load is applied.

This mechanism defines income as directional movement into the system and liquidity as already-held absorption capacity within the system. Income may be sufficient in aggregate yet unavailable at the required interval. Liquidity solves a different structural problem: it bridges the gap between ongoing demand and the timing of replenishment. The two are related components of total capacity, but they perform different operational roles.

Across time, systems with strong income but weak liquidity may still experience short-term instability because incoming flow cannot absorb load that arrives before it does. Stable systems do not confuse flow with immediate availability. Depleted systems often rely on future inflow to solve present load, which leaves them exposed at the point of interaction. This difference becomes especially visible under timing mismatch, variability, and shock.

The contrast shows that income determines replenishment rate, while liquidity determines immediate absorbability. A system may appear strong on a flow basis and remain fragile on a liquidity basis. Liquidity versus income therefore defines the difference between eventual capacity and present capacity.

Liquidity as short-term capacity means that it determines whether the system can remain stable at the exact interval load is applied. This makes liquidity the operative form of capacity in immediate system conditions. Income contributes to total capacity, but liquidity decides whether that capacity exists in usable form at the current point of demand. In structural terms, liquidity governs present stability.

This mechanism defines short-term capacity as the amount of demand the system can absorb now rather than later. Liquidity performs this function because it is already accessible and does not depend on future sequence. When expenses are applied, the system must respond with available resources, not anticipated resources. Liquidity therefore converts capacity from a theoretical total into an operational quantity.

Across time, short-term capacity determines how the system experiences ordinary outflow. Stable systems maintain enough immediate absorptive ability that routine expenses do not create pressure simply because of sequence. Depleted systems may have adequate expected inflow yet insufficient short-term capacity, causing ordinary demand to generate instability. This gap between total capacity and current absorptive capacity is what makes liquidity central to system resilience.

The contrast is decisive. Systems with strong short-term capacity absorb load continuously, while systems with weak short-term capacity depend on timing precision or external correction. Liquidity as short-term capacity therefore defines whether the system can meet demand at the moment demand arrives.

Expenses as liquidity draw means that every outflow consumes part of the system's immediately available absorptive capacity. When load is applied, liquidity is reduced in proportion to the amount not offset instantly by inflow. This makes expenses the direct mechanism through which stored capacity is converted into depletion. The expense system does not merely record outflow; it translates outflow into reduced future absorbability.

This mechanism defines liquidity draw as the consumption of accessible reserves by active demand. Each expense event reduces what remains available to absorb later load. Even when this reduction is temporary and later replenished, it still alters the system's short-term condition between intervals. Liquidity is therefore not a passive background asset but an actively consumed resource under ongoing outflow.

Across time, repeated expense application creates a continuous relationship between load and available reserves. Stable systems experience draw that is proportional, expected, and replenishable, preventing cumulative depletion. Depleted systems experience draw that outpaces replenishment, reducing available capacity from one interval to the next. This produces a progressively weaker short-term position even without dramatic changes in total expense level.

The contrast shows that expenses do not only create pressure when they exceed total capacity. They also erode the liquidity layer that prevents future pressure. Expenses as liquidity draw therefore explains why routine outflow has cumulative structural significance even before formal breakdown occurs.

Continuous liquidity interaction means that expenses and liquidity affect each other across every interval, not only during obvious stress events. Outflow is continuously consuming available capacity, while inflow is continuously restoring or failing to restore it. This makes liquidity a dynamic resource rather than a static reserve. The expense system is therefore always in an active state of capacity consumption and replenishment.

This mechanism defines liquidity interaction as ongoing rather than episodic. Each expense changes the immediately available absorption level, and each period of inflow changes what capacity is restored. The system's condition at any moment depends on the sequence of these interactions rather than on isolated snapshots. Liquidity must be understood through movement, not through nominal balances alone.

Across time, stable systems maintain continuity because ongoing draw and replenishment remain roughly aligned. Liquidity declines during expense application but does not trend downward persistently because restoration keeps pace with use. Depleted systems show a different pattern:

each round of outflow leaves less immediately available capacity than before, even if no single interval appears catastrophic. This gradual weakening creates a structurally more fragile short-term position.

The contrast highlights that liquidity interaction is not exceptional; it is the ordinary operating condition of the system. Systems that sustain stable interaction preserve absorptive capacity. Systems with deteriorating interaction experience cumulative depletion. Continuous liquidity interaction therefore defines how everyday expense behavior shapes short-term system stability.

Liquidity drawdown occurs when expenses exceed immediately available inflow and the system must consume stored capacity to maintain continuity. This mechanism converts imbalance into reserve usage rather than immediate failure. Drawdown is the operational process by which liquidity absorbs the gap between current load and current flow. It is the system's internal bridging response to short-term insufficiency.

This mechanism defines drawdown as reserve consumption triggered by interval-level imbalance. When load cannot be met entirely by current inflow, the system uses liquidity to preserve continuity. Drawdown is not itself collapse; it is the buffer function operating under strain. But repeated drawdown without adequate restoration converts temporary support into structural depletion.

Across time, drawdown reveals whether the system is using liquidity as occasional support or as a recurring substitute for insufficient operating alignment. Stable systems draw down liquidity in contained and recoverable ways, allowing replenishment to restore capacity between periods. Depleted systems rely on drawdown repeatedly, causing reserves to trend downward across intervals. In those systems, liquidity is no longer buffering exceptions; it is compensating for ongoing structural mismatch.

The contrast is structural rather than emotional. Occasional drawdown within a replenishing system preserves stability, while persistent drawdown within a non-replenishing system erodes future capacity.

Drawdown mechanics therefore explain how short-term imbalance becomes cumulative depletion.

Liquidity versus pressure defines the relationship between reserve depletion and the likelihood that load will exceed available capacity. Pressure forms when the system can no longer absorb current demand, and declining liquidity moves the system closer to that condition with each interval. Liquidity therefore does not eliminate pressure permanently; it delays or absorbs it until reserves thin out. The level of remaining liquidity determines how close the system is to active imbalance.

This mechanism defines liquidity as the layer that prevents ordinary load from becoming immediate pressure. When liquidity is present, timing gaps, variable spikes, and modest shortfalls can be absorbed without overt breakdown. When liquidity is depleted, the same conditions generate pressure more quickly because less immediate capacity remains. Depletion therefore changes the threshold at which pressure appears.

Across time, stable systems preserve enough liquidity that pressure remains episodic or contained. Depleted systems lose that reserve layer, causing pressure to emerge under smaller deviations and with greater frequency. This creates a shift in system behavior: conditions that were once manageable now become destabilizing. Liquidity decline thus changes the operating threshold even if total expense levels have not dramatically changed.

The contrast shows that liquidity and pressure are linked through absorptive distance. Systems with strong liquidity keep pressure formation farther away. Systems with weak liquidity operate near the pressure boundary at all times. Liquidity versus pressure therefore defines how reserve depletion converts normal load into instability risk.

Sustained outflow and depletion are linked because continuous expenses reduce liquidity whenever ongoing demand is not fully matched by replenishing inflow. Depletion emerges not only from isolated large events but from persistent net consumption of available capacity across time. This means a system can weaken structurally through ordinary repetition rather than through extraordinary disruption. Sustained outflow is therefore a primary engine of liquidity decline.

This mechanism defines depletion as cumulative reserve reduction under repeated net outflow. Each interval of demand that is not fully restored by incoming capacity leaves the system with less absorbable capacity for future intervals. What matters is not whether any single expense is large, but whether total outflow repeatedly consumes more accessible capacity than is restored. This makes depletion a temporal process rather than a momentary event.

Across time, stable systems may experience sustained outflow without depletion if replenishment reliably restores the liquidity consumed. Depleted systems experience the opposite pattern: each cycle leaves reserves lower than before, creating a gradual downward slope in short-term capacity. The system becomes less resilient with each iteration because continued operation depends on a shrinking resource base.

The contrast shows that sustained outflow is not neutral merely because it appears routine. In one system it is matched and reversible; in another it is cumulative and erosive. Sustained outflow and depletion therefore explain how persistent expenses transform stored capacity into long-term fragility.

Liquidity buffer function is the role liquidity plays in absorbing temporary imbalance before that imbalance becomes pressure or stress. It provides immediate capacity that allows the system to continue operating when load and inflow are misaligned. This makes liquidity not just a reserve, but a structural stabilizer of short-term system behavior. Its function is absorptive before it is merely accumulative.

This mechanism defines the buffer as the reserve layer that stands between ordinary deviation and overt instability. When variability increases, timing shifts occur, or small shocks arrive, liquidity absorbs the resulting gap. This prevents the system from moving instantly from deviation to pressure. The buffer function therefore transforms potentially destabilizing conditions into manageable load events.

Across time, stable systems retain enough liquidity for this buffer function to remain intact. Depleted systems may still possess nominal reserves, but once those reserves are too thin to absorb common deviations, the buffer function has effectively weakened. At that point, the system reacts more sharply to ordinary disturbances because reserve absorption is no longer sufficient. The issue is not simply reserve presence, but reserve adequacy relative to the system's demand pattern.

The contrast shows that liquidity matters because of what it prevents. Systems with a functioning buffer maintain continuity under irregular conditions. Systems with a compromised buffer convert ordinary deviations into repeated pressure. Liquidity buffer function therefore defines how reserves preserve short-term stability.

Depletion without replenishment emerges when the system consumes liquidity repeatedly without restoring the reserves that have been used. This produces structural decline in short-term capacity because each interval begins from a lower reserve base than the one before. The system does not fail all at once; it weakens through cumulative non-restoration. This makes replenishment as structurally important as drawdown.

This mechanism defines non-replenished depletion as a directional process of reserve contraction. Drawdown alone does not guarantee instability if restoration follows. The destabilizing condition appears when used liquidity is not rebuilt, causing the reserve layer to thin progressively over time. The system then becomes dependent on a resource that is being consumed faster than it is renewed.

Across time, stable systems experience periods of drawdown but return toward prior reserve levels, preserving their absorptive function. Depleted systems remain in a downward trajectory, where each round of expense application takes place against a weaker liquidity base. This affects not just current stability but future response capacity, because smaller reserves make later outflows more destabilizing.

The contrast is structural and cumulative. Systems with replenishment retain operational resilience, while systems without replenishment lose it gradually but continuously. Depletion without replenishment therefore defines the mechanism by which short-term capacity erodes into chronic instability.

Liquidity and timing mismatch are linked because liquidity is the resource that bridges intervals where load arrives before income becomes available. Timing mismatch does not always imply total insufficiency; it often reflects sequence failure between outflow and inflow. Liquidity allows the system to absorb that sequence gap without immediate pressure. In this role, liquidity converts delayed capacity into usable continuity.

This mechanism defines liquidity as a sequencing bridge rather than a substitute for income in general. When expenses occur before inflow, stored capacity absorbs the interim load. This prevents ordinary sequencing gaps from becoming explicit instability events. The bridge function is therefore central to systems where flow timing and load timing are not perfectly aligned.

Across time, stable systems use liquidity to bridge occasional mismatch while preserving enough reserves for continued short-term capacity. Depleted systems face a different pattern: because reserves are already thin, timing mismatches produce faster pressure and more frequent strain. The same sequence gap has different consequences depending on the remaining liquidity available to bridge it. This is why sequence stability cannot be understood apart from stored capacity.

The contrast shows that timing mismatch is manageable in one system and destabilizing in another not because the sequence differs, but because bridging ability differs. Liquidity and timing mismatch therefore define the connection between sequence failure and reserve dependence.

Liquidity under variability refers to how fluctuating load patterns accelerate reserve consumption by producing intervals of elevated demand that exceed ordinary inflow support. Variability does not need to be extreme to matter; it only needs to create repeated deviations large enough to require stored capacity. Liquidity becomes the absorber of those fluctuations whenever current flow is insufficient. This makes variability a major accelerator of depletion.

This mechanism defines variable load as an amplifier of drawdown frequency and intensity. Under stable distribution, reserve use may remain limited because load is predictable and absorbable within ordinary operating conditions. Under fluctuating distribution, however, the system encounters more frequent peaks that require reserve support. Liquidity is therefore consumed not only by high averages, but by irregular load behavior.

Across time, stable systems contain variability within a range that liquidity can absorb without directional decline. Depleted systems experience variability as a reserve-draining pattern because fluctuations repeatedly exceed current absorptive flow. This causes reserves to fall more quickly even when average expenses are not dramatically higher. The result is that irregularity itself becomes a depletion driver.

The contrast shows that variability changes the rate at which liquidity is consumed. Systems with bounded fluctuation preserve reserves more effectively, while systems with unstable fluctuation draw them down repeatedly. Liquidity under variability therefore explains how pattern instability converts into reserve erosion.

Liquidity under shock refers to the way sudden load spikes force rapid consumption of stored capacity within a single interval. Because shock introduces abrupt demand that current inflow cannot usually absorb immediately, liquidity becomes the primary resource used to contain the event. This makes shock one of the fastest pathways to accelerated drawdown. The reserve layer is tested in compressed time.

This mechanism defines shock drawdown as concentrated reserve consumption caused by discrete load increase. Unlike ordinary variability, which may spread depletion across intervals, shock can remove a significant portion of short-term capacity at once. The system's response depends on how much immediately available capacity exists before the event. Shock therefore reveals not only the presence of liquidity but the adequacy of liquidity under acute demand.

Across time, stable systems absorb shocks without exhausting their reserve function because available liquidity remains large enough relative to the event. Depleted systems experience a different result: a single shock can materially weaken or exhaust their remaining short-term capacity, leaving them exposed in later intervals. In such systems, the problem is not only the shock itself but the altered post-shock reserve condition.

The contrast shows that shock is not destabilizing solely because it is sudden. It is destabilizing because it compresses reserve consumption into a narrow interval. Liquidity under shock therefore defines how acute load events translate into immediate capacity erosion.

Liquidity erosion over time is the cumulative reduction of immediately available capacity across repeated intervals of drawdown, incomplete replenishment, or both. It is the long-term expression of ongoing reserve consumption under expense pressure. Rather than appearing as one dramatic collapse, erosion appears as a thinning of the system's absorptive layer. This makes the system progressively less tolerant even when no single interval appears catastrophic.

This mechanism defines erosion as cumulative directional weakening of reserve capacity. Each episode of drawdown that is not fully restored leaves the system with less immediate resilience than before. Over time, this changes the system's response profile: smaller deviations produce larger effects because less liquidity remains to absorb them. Erosion therefore alters not just quantity of reserves but quality of system stability.

Across time, stable systems may use liquidity regularly without exhibiting erosion because replenishment and bounded load preserve reserve levels. Depleted systems experience a different trajectory, where reserves trend downward and short-term capacity becomes progressively thinner. This creates a silent instability pattern: the system seems functional until ordinary variation begins generating repeated pressure due to weakened absorption.

The contrast shows that erosion is not merely balance decline. It is a structural loss of short-term stabilizing capacity. Liquidity erosion over time therefore defines how routine expense behavior can gradually undermine the system's ability to remain stable.

Expenses as primary driver of depletion means that outflows are the direct mechanism through which liquidity declines across time. Inflow replenishes, but outflow determines the rate and frequency of reserve consumption. This places expenses at the center of liquidity dynamics rather than treating depletion as an abstract reserve problem. Liquidity falls because load continuously draws against it.

This mechanism defines depletion as load-driven rather than independently occurring. Every time expenses exceed the immediately absorbable level of current inflow, liquidity must cover the difference. Repeated outflow therefore determines whether reserves remain stable, erode slowly, or decline rapidly. The system's depletion pattern is fundamentally an expense pattern translated into reserve terms.

Across time, stable systems maintain expense structures that do not force persistent reserve use beyond replenishment capacity. Depleted systems do the opposite: their outflow patterns repeatedly consume more immediate capacity than is restored, causing liquidity decline to become structural. This remains true whether the cause is baseline pressure, variability, timing mismatch, or shock. In every case, expenses are the mechanism that converts system demand into reserve erosion.

The contrast makes the chapter's core point explicit. Liquidity depletion is not an independent financial event that happens alongside expenses. It is the direct consequence of how expenses interact with available short-term capacity. Expenses as primary driver of depletion therefore defines why outflow is the central force in the erosion of liquidity.

Expenses and Runway

Runway is defined as the duration the system can sustain expense load using available liquidity when inflow is reduced or absent. It converts stored capacity into time by expressing how long the system can continue operating under current demand conditions. This establishes runway as a temporal property rather than a static resource level.

This mechanism defines runway as dependent on both liquidity and expenses, but not identical to either. Liquidity provides the resource base, while expenses determine the rate at which that base is consumed. Runway therefore exists only as a function of depletion over time.

Across time, runway continuously declines as expenses draw down liquidity. Stable systems maintain longer durations because depletion occurs at a controlled rate relative to available reserves. Short-runway systems experience rapid decline in remaining duration due to higher or less controlled load.

The contrast shows that runway is not determined by reserves alone. Systems with identical liquidity can have different runway depending on expense structure. Runway therefore defines how long capacity can sustain load under ongoing consumption.

Runway as time-to-failure refers to the point at which liquidity is fully exhausted and the system can no longer sustain expense load without inflow. This defines runway as a countdown toward a structural endpoint rather than an indefinite buffer.

This mechanism defines time-to-failure as the terminal condition of depletion. As expenses consume liquidity across intervals, the system moves progressively closer to this endpoint. Runway measures the remaining distance to that failure point in time units rather than in resource units.

Across time, systems with longer runway approach failure gradually, allowing extended operation under reduced or absent inflow. Systems with shorter runway approach failure rapidly, with little tolerance for disruption. The rate of approach is determined by expense-driven depletion.

The contrast highlights that runway is inherently directional. It always moves toward zero unless replenishment offsets consumption. Long-runway systems maintain extended duration before failure, while short-runway systems face imminent depletion. Runway as time-to-failure therefore defines the system's remaining operational horizon.

The liquidity-runway relationship defines how stored capacity is translated into time through the rate of expense consumption. Liquidity represents the quantity of available resources, while runway represents how long those resources last under current load conditions.

This mechanism defines runway as a derived measure rather than a direct resource. The same level of liquidity produces different runway durations depending on expense levels. Liquidity is static in quantity, but runway is dynamic in duration.

Across time, systems with identical liquidity but different expense rates experience different runway trajectories. Stable systems convert liquidity into extended duration through controlled depletion. Unstable systems convert the same liquidity into shorter duration because of higher or more irregular load.

The contrast shows that liquidity alone does not determine survival time. The interaction between liquidity and expenses defines how quickly reserves are consumed. The liquidity-runway relationship therefore explains how stored capacity becomes a time-based constraint.

Expenses as runway driver means that load determines the rate at which liquidity is consumed and therefore how quickly runway declines. Higher expenses accelerate depletion, while lower expenses slow it. This establishes expenses as the primary control on survival duration.

This mechanism defines expenses as the rate component of runway. While liquidity defines the starting quantity, expenses define the speed at which that quantity is reduced. Runway is therefore a function of consumption velocity applied to available reserves.

Across time, systems with higher expense levels experience rapid reduction in remaining runway. Stable systems maintain lower or more controlled expense structures, preserving duration. Short-runway systems consume liquidity quickly, reducing their time horizon.

The contrast highlights that runway is not fixed by initial reserves. It is continuously reshaped by expense behavior. Systems with identical liquidity can diverge significantly in survival time depending on load. Expenses as runway driver therefore defines the rate-based nature of system endurance.

Runway as a rate-based condition means that survival duration is determined by the continuous interaction between expense rate and available liquidity. It is not an instant condition but an ongoing process of depletion over time.

This mechanism defines runway as dependent on flow dynamics rather than static balance. The system does not fail because liquidity reaches zero instantly, but because it is consumed progressively through expense application. This makes time an essential variable in system stability.

Across time, runway declines incrementally with each interval of outflow. Stable systems manage this decline by maintaining controlled rates of consumption. Unstable systems experience accelerated decline due to elevated or irregular expense rates.

The contrast shows that runway cannot be evaluated at a single point without considering rate. Systems with slow depletion maintain extended duration, while systems with rapid depletion compress their survival window. Runway as a rate-based condition therefore defines how time and load interact to determine system endurance.

Runway compression emerges when elevated expenses increase the rate of liquidity depletion, reducing the time the system can sustain operation. Higher load accelerates movement toward time-to-failure, shortening available duration.

This mechanism defines compression as a function of increased consumption velocity. When expenses rise, liquidity is consumed more quickly, causing runway to decline at a faster rate. This reduces the system's tolerance to disruption.

Across time, high-expense systems experience rapid contraction of remaining runway. Stable systems maintain lower or controlled expense levels, preserving longer duration. Short-runway systems see their operational horizon shrink quickly under sustained high load.

The contrast highlights that compression is driven by rate, not just magnitude. Systems with high expenses consume reserves quickly, while systems with lower expenses extend duration. High expenses and runway compression therefore define how elevated load reduces survival time.

Runway expansion occurs when reduced expenses decrease the rate of liquidity depletion, extending the duration the system can sustain load. Lower consumption slows the approach to time-to-failure, increasing survival time.

This mechanism defines expansion as a reduction in depletion velocity. When expenses are lower, liquidity lasts longer because it is consumed more gradually. This increases the system's time horizon without requiring additional resources.

Across time, low-expense systems maintain longer runway because each interval consumes a smaller portion of available liquidity. Stable systems preserve duration through controlled load. Short-runway systems fail to achieve expansion because of higher expense levels.

The contrast shows that expansion is not driven by increased liquidity alone. It can also result from reduced consumption rate. Systems with lower expenses extend their operational duration relative to their reserves. Low expenses and runway expansion therefore define how reduced load increases survival time.

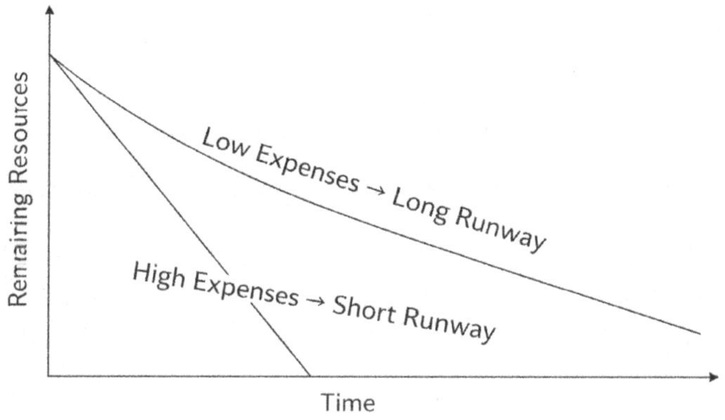

[Figure 11: Expenses vs Runway — higher expenses shorten survival time]

Runway sensitivity to load changes refers to how small variations in expenses can significantly alter survival duration. Because runway is rate-based, even minor adjustments in load can produce meaningful changes in time-to-failure.

This mechanism defines sensitivity as a proportional response of duration to changes in expense rate. When expenses increase slightly, depletion accelerates and runway shortens. When expenses decrease slightly, depletion slows and runway extends.

Across time, sensitive systems exhibit noticeable changes in runway from relatively small shifts in load. Stable systems maintain controlled expense levels to avoid large swings in duration. Unstable systems experience significant variation in runway due to fluctuating load.

The contrast highlights that runway is highly responsive to rate changes. Systems with stable load maintain predictable duration, while systems with variable load experience shifting survival horizons. Runway sensitivity to load changes therefore defines how small variations affect time-based stability.

Runway under zero inflow represents the condition where no new capacity enters the system and all expenses must be sustained entirely through liquidity. This creates a pure depletion model in which runway declines continuously until reserves are exhausted.

This mechanism defines zero-inflow runway as a closed system with no replenishment. The only variable determining duration is the rate of expense consumption relative to available liquidity. This isolates the relationship between load and stored capacity.

Across time, zero-inflow systems experience steady decline in runway as liquidity is consumed. Stable systems with lower expense rates maintain longer duration. Short-runway systems reach time-to-failure quickly because of higher consumption rates.

The contrast shows that without inflow, survival time depends entirely on existing reserves and expense rate. Systems with lower load extend duration, while systems with higher load compress it. Runway under zero inflow therefore defines the baseline depletion scenario.

Runway under partial inflow occurs when incoming capacity offsets some but not all expenses, reducing the rate of liquidity depletion. This extends survival duration relative to zero-inflow conditions but does not eliminate depletion entirely.

This mechanism defines partial inflow as a moderating factor on consumption rate. When inflow partially covers expenses, less liquidity is consumed per interval. This slows the decline in runway but does not stop it unless inflow fully matches load.

Across time, systems with partial inflow experience gradual reduction in runway rather than immediate depletion. Stable systems maintain longer duration due to reduced net consumption. Short-runway systems still face decline, but at a slower rate.

The contrast highlights that partial inflow alters the slope of depletion rather than eliminating it. Systems with sufficient inflow maintain stable or slowly declining runway, while those with insufficient inflow continue to lose duration. Runway under partial inflow therefore defines moderated depletion dynamics.

Runway and variability are linked because fluctuations in expenses change the rate of liquidity depletion across intervals. Variability introduces periods of higher consumption that accelerate the reduction of runway.

This mechanism defines variability as a modifier of depletion rate. When expenses fluctuate, periods of elevated load consume more liquidity than average, compressing runway more quickly than stable patterns would suggest.

Across time, systems with high variability experience uneven decline in runway, with sharp reductions during peak intervals. Stable systems maintain consistent depletion rates, preserving predictable duration. Unstable systems see accelerated loss of runway due to irregular load.

The contrast shows that variability affects not just total consumption but the pattern of depletion. Systems with stable load maintain steady runway decline, while systems with fluctuating load experience faster erosion. Runway and variability therefore define how fluctuation impacts survival time.

Runway and timing mismatch are connected because sequencing gaps can force earlier or more frequent liquidity usage, effectively reducing usable survival duration. When expenses occur before inflow, reserves must be used sooner.

This mechanism defines timing mismatch as altering when depletion occurs rather than how much total depletion happens. Early or repeated drawdowns reduce available liquidity sooner, compressing effective runway.

Across time, systems with aligned timing maintain smoother depletion patterns and preserve runway. Systems with mismatched timing consume liquidity earlier and more frequently, reducing remaining duration.

The contrast highlights that sequencing affects effective survival time. Systems with aligned load and inflow maintain longer usable runway, while misaligned systems experience earlier depletion. Runway and timing mismatch therefore define how sequence influences duration.

Runway under shock refers to the immediate reduction in survival duration caused by sudden increases in expense load. Shock events consume liquidity rapidly, compressing runway within a single interval.

This mechanism defines shock as a discrete acceleration of depletion. When load spikes, a large portion of liquidity is consumed at once, reducing remaining runway abruptly. This shortens the time-to-failure.

Across time, systems with sufficient liquidity absorb shocks with limited impact on runway. Stable systems maintain enough reserves to withstand sudden depletion. Short-runway systems experience significant compression from even a single shock.

The contrast shows that shock affects both magnitude and timing of depletion. Systems with larger reserves maintain duration, while systems with limited reserves lose runway quickly. Runway under shock therefore defines how sudden load reduces survival time.

Runway degradation over time refers to the continuous reduction of remaining survival duration as expenses are applied across intervals. Each period of outflow reduces both liquidity and the time the system can continue operating. Runway therefore declines not as a discrete event but as an ongoing process of consumption.

This mechanism defines degradation as cumulative decline in duration. Runway is not static; it decreases with each unit of consumption unless replenishment offsets depletion. The system does not lose time suddenly but progressively, creating a downward trajectory in remaining duration.

Across time, stable systems experience gradual degradation with predictable decline because expenses and reserves remain proportionally aligned. Unstable systems experience accelerated degradation due to higher or irregular expenses, causing survival duration to contract more quickly. The rate of degradation reflects the interaction between load and available reserves.

The contrast shows that degradation is inherent to any system relying on finite liquidity, but the rate determines stability. Systems with controlled load decline slowly and remain operational for extended periods, while systems with elevated load lose duration rapidly and approach failure sooner. Runway degradation over time therefore defines how survival duration diminishes under sustained expenses.

Runway as a stability constraint means that limited survival duration restricts the system's ability to absorb disruption and maintain continuity. When runway is short, the system operates under time pressure, increasing sensitivity to variability, timing mismatch, and shock.

This mechanism defines runway as a temporal boundary on stability. It determines how long imbalance can be tolerated before failure occurs. Systems with extended runway have time to absorb disruption and recover, while systems with limited runway must remain tightly aligned or face rapid breakdown.

Across time, long-runway systems maintain resilience because duration allows for adjustment, recovery, and absorption of irregular conditions.

Short-runway systems become fragile because even minor deviations accelerate depletion and reduce remaining survival time.

The contrast shows that available time determines system tolerance to disruption. Systems with sufficient runway maintain stability under changing conditions, while systems with limited runway operate near failure and react sharply to disturbance. Runway as a stability constraint therefore defines the temporal limits of system resilience.

Expenses vs. Income Variability

Income variability is defined as fluctuation in inflow magnitude and timing across intervals. It refers to changes in how much capacity enters the system and when that capacity becomes available. This makes income variability distinct from expense variability, which alters load rather than inflow. Within the system model, income variability changes the reliability of replenishment rather than the level of demand.

This mechanism defines inflow instability as a structural problem of uncertain support. When income changes in size or arrives at irregular intervals, the system cannot assume that future capacity will match current expectations. This alters how much short-term stability can be maintained without reserve use. Income variability therefore weakens the predictability of the capacity side of the system.

Across time, systems with stable inflow can align load against a relatively reliable replenishment pattern. Systems with variable inflow face a different condition, where even unchanged expenses may generate pressure because support arrives inconsistently or at reduced levels. The instability appears not because load has changed, but because the timing and scale of replenishment have changed. Income variability thus becomes an independent source of structural uncertainty.

The contrast shows that not all instability begins on the expense side. A system may have controlled load and still experience instability if inflow becomes unreliable. Income variability therefore defines fluctuation in the support layer that sustains ongoing system operation.

Expense variability versus income variability distinguishes instability in load from instability in inflow. Expense variability alters the demand applied to the system, while income variability alters the support available to absorb that demand. These are separate mechanisms because they affect opposite sides of the load-capacity relationship. One changes what must be absorbed; the other changes what is available to absorb it.

This mechanism defines expense variability as fluctuation in outflow magnitude and timing, and income variability as fluctuation in inflow magnitude and timing. The system can experience either type independently. A system with stable income may still face irregular demand, and a system with stable expenses may still face irregular replenishment. Their structural effects differ even though both increase instability.

Across time, expense variability produces uncertainty in load application, while income variability produces uncertainty in capacity restoration. Stable systems may tolerate one form of variability if the opposite side remains relatively steady. But system behavior changes depending on which side fluctuates. Load-side instability pressures absorptive capacity from above, while inflow-side instability weakens the replenishment base from below.

The contrast clarifies why the two mechanisms cannot be merged into a single generic concept of instability. Expense variability and income variability are distinct because they alter different structural elements. Their distinction becomes critical once both begin operating simultaneously.

Independent variability effects refer to the instability produced when either load or inflow fluctuates while the opposite side remains relatively stable. This defines single-variable instability as a condition in which one system component introduces uncertainty without requiring both to do so. The effect can still be significant, but it remains structurally limited to one side of the equation.

This mechanism defines expense-only variability as a demand problem and income-only variability as a replenishment problem. In the first case, the system must absorb uneven load against relatively stable support. In the second case, the system must sustain steady demand against uneven support. Either pattern can generate pressure, liquidity use, and stress without requiring simultaneous instability on both sides.

Across time, single-variable systems may preserve partial predictability because one side remains stable enough to anchor system behavior. Stable inflow can offset irregular load more effectively than unstable inflow can, and stable expenses allow irregular income to be modeled against a fixed demand floor. The presence of one reliable side reduces the range of possible deviations. This does not eliminate instability, but it constrains it.

The contrast shows why single-variable instability is serious but not maximal. Systems with one stable side retain a structural anchor. Systems with instability on both sides lose that anchor. Independent variability effects therefore define the limited but still meaningful instability that arises when only one component fluctuates.

Dual variability emerges when both expense load and income inflow fluctuate at the same time. This creates simultaneous instability in demand and support, removing the structural reliability that single-variable systems still retain. The system no longer faces isolated uncertainty; it faces interacting uncertainty across both sides of the balance. This is the defining condition of compounded instability.

This mechanism defines dual variability as coexisting fluctuation in outflow and inflow magnitude, timing, or both. Because the system cannot rely on either side to remain stable, each interval contains a wider set of possible load-capacity outcomes. Demand may spike when inflow weakens, or inflow may arrive late when expenses cluster. This makes the system harder to stabilize through ordinary alignment.

Across time, dual-variable systems experience instability not only more often but with less predictability. Stable systems can often recover because one side remains reliable enough to absorb or offset movement on the other side. Under dual variability, that stabilizing counterweight is missing. Each cycle becomes more exposed to mismatch, reserve dependence, and pressure events.

The contrast highlights that dual variability is not simply a larger amount of the same problem. It changes the system from partially uncertain to structurally uncertain on both sides. The dual-variability condition therefore defines the threshold where instability becomes interactive rather than isolated.

Interaction effects in system behavior occur when variability on one side of the system changes the impact of variability on the other side. This means that expense instability and income instability do not merely coexist; they influence how strongly each other is felt. The system's outcome becomes a product of interaction rather than simple co-presence. This is the mechanism that transforms dual variability into compounded instability.

This mechanism defines interaction as cross-effect between fluctuating variables. A spike in expenses is more destabilizing when inflow is simultaneously weak or delayed. Likewise, an inflow shortfall is more damaging when expenses are already elevated or irregular. The effect of each variable depends partly on the state of the other.

Across time, interaction effects widen the gap between expected and actual system performance. Single-variable systems may still produce relatively bounded deviations because one stable side dampens the moving side. Dual-variable systems amplify deviations because instability on one side removes the system's ability to counter instability on the other. As a result, outcomes become more volatile and less recoverable.

The contrast shows that interaction is structurally different from coincidence. Two unstable variables operating independently produce one kind of risk. Two unstable variables altering each other's impact produce a more complex and amplified kind of risk. Interaction effects in system behavior therefore define how dual variability becomes systemically more dangerous than isolated fluctuation.

Additive versus multiplicative instability distinguishes linear risk accumulation from amplified interaction risk. Additive instability means that expense variability and income variability contribute separate, independent burdens to the system. Multiplicative instability means that their combination produces effects larger than their separate contributions would suggest. This difference defines whether the system remains linearly stressed or becomes nonlinearly unstable.

This mechanism defines additive risk as independent contribution without interaction amplification. If unstable expenses add one layer of pressure and unstable income adds another, the total effect remains roughly the sum of both. Multiplicative risk appears when the instability of one variable intensifies the destabilizing effect of the other. The result is not one-plus-one, but a larger structural escalation.

Across time, additive systems remain difficult but somewhat more predictable because the burdens can be approximated separately. Multiplicative systems behave differently. Pressure appears more frequently, liquidity is consumed faster, and runway shortens more abruptly because the interaction produces nonlinear outcomes. Small changes on one side can trigger outsized effects because the other side is already unstable.

The contrast shows that multiplicative instability is not just severe variability. It is a different structural regime in which variable forces reinforce each other's damage. Additive versus multiplicative instability therefore defines the transition from combined stress to amplified system fragility.

Amplification of timing mismatch occurs when variability in both expenses and income increases the frequency and severity of sequencing gaps between load and inflow. Timing mismatch already creates instability when expenses arrive before support. Under dual variability, both the load sequence and the replenishment sequence become unreliable. This makes sequencing failure more likely and more destabilizing when it occurs.

This mechanism defines amplified mismatch as misalignment under uncertainty on both sides of the interval. Expenses may arrive earlier, in larger amounts, or in more irregular clusters just as inflow arrives later, in reduced amounts, or with more irregular timing. The system loses the stabilizing assumption that one side will remain sequenced reliably even if the other side shifts. This expands the number of adverse interval combinations.

Across time, systems with single-sided variability may still maintain enough sequence reliability to limit reserve use. Under dual variability, sequencing gaps become harder to predict and harder to bridge because both arrival patterns are unstable. Liquidity must absorb more mismatches, and pressure events begin from smaller deviations. The system becomes more sensitive not merely to amount, but to order.

The contrast shows that timing mismatch under dual variability is not the same as timing mismatch under otherwise stable conditions. It becomes deeper, more frequent, and less containable. Amplification of timing mismatch therefore defines how sequencing risk escalates when both load and inflow become unstable together.

Pressure formation under dual variability refers to the increased frequency and intensity of interval-level imbalance when both demand and support fluctuate simultaneously. Pressure arises whenever load exceeds available capacity at a given interval. Under dual variability, that threshold is crossed more often because both sides are moving unpredictably. This changes pressure from episodic exception to recurrent operating condition.

This mechanism defines dual-variable pressure as more than the sum of expense spikes and inflow shortfalls. The system does not merely face occasional high load or occasional weak inflow. It faces the possibility that both occur together, and that their interaction erodes the reliability of each interval's balance. This produces more frequent breaches of available short-term capacity.

Across time, stable or single-variable systems may contain pressure because one side remains sufficiently predictable to offset the other. Dual-variable systems lose that stabilizing structure. Pressure not only appears more often, but may arrive in larger bursts because adverse expense and income conditions align within the same interval. This increases both event frequency and event severity.

The contrast shows why pressure behaves differently under compound fluctuation. Systems with only one unstable side retain some absorptive predictability. Systems with two unstable sides operate closer to repeated imbalance by design. Pressure formation under dual variability therefore defines the interval-level manifestation of compounded instability.

Liquidity dependence under dual variability means that the system must rely more heavily on buffer capacity because neither load nor inflow can be trusted to remain stable. Liquidity becomes the balancing mechanism when fluctuating expenses and fluctuating income fail to align. This increases not only reserve use, but reserve importance within the system's structure. The buffer layer carries more of the system's operating burden.

This mechanism defines dual-variable reserve dependence as repeated use of stored capacity to compensate for uncertainty on both sides. A system with stable inflow or stable expenses may need liquidity only occasionally. Under dual variability, reserve use becomes more frequent because load and support are both unreliable. Liquidity shifts from secondary absorber to central stabilizer.

Across time, this heavier dependence accelerates depletion pressure. Stable systems preserve liquidity because one side of the system remains predictable enough to reduce reserve bridging. Dual-variable systems consume liquidity more persistently, leaving less absorptive capacity for future intervals. This creates a feedback pattern where reserve use increases precisely as reserve adequacy declines.

The contrast shows that liquidity in dual-variable systems is not merely helpful; it becomes structurally necessary. Systems with one stable side may use reserves tactically. Systems with both sides unstable use reserves continuously and more aggressively. Liquidity dependence under dual variability therefore defines the increased burden placed on stored capacity when uncertainty exists across both demand and inflow.

Runway compression under dual variability occurs when interacting instability in expenses and income accelerates liquidity depletion and shortens time-to-failure more quickly than either variable would alone. Runway is always a function of reserves and depletion rate. When both the depletion rate and the replenishment pattern become unstable, remaining duration contracts faster and with less predictability. This makes the system's survival horizon more fragile.

This mechanism defines compounded runway compression as a time-based effect of interacting uncertainty. Expense variability raises or concentrates consumption, while income variability weakens or delays replenishment. Together they cause reserves to fall faster and more erratically. The resulting loss of runway is not merely gradual decline, but accelerated compression under interacting stress.

Across time, systems with stable inflow or stable load may still project duration with some confidence. Dual-variable systems cannot do so reliably because each interval can alter both net consumption and reserve restoration in adverse ways. This causes remaining runway to shorten in sharper steps and to recover less often. The system loses not only duration, but confidence in duration.

The contrast shows that runway under dual variability is different from runway under simple depletion. It is shorter, more unstable, and more sensitive to interval-level interaction. Runway compression under dual variability therefore defines how time-to-failure is accelerated when both sides of the system become unreliable together.

Variability synchronization risk is the danger that adverse expense variability and adverse income variability occur in the same interval or sequence of intervals. This produces concentrated instability because the system faces elevated load precisely when support is reduced or delayed. The problem is not merely that both variables fluctuate, but that they can fluctuate unfavorably at the same time. This alignment creates especially damaging system states.

This mechanism defines synchronization risk as coincident adverse movement across both variables. An expense spike by itself may be manageable, and an inflow dip by itself may be manageable. When they align, the system loses both absorptive room and replenishment reliability at once. This creates deeper pressure events than unsynchronized variability would.

Across time, synchronization events tend to compress liquidity and runway disproportionately because the system must bridge larger gaps with fewer compensating inflow resources. Stable systems are less exposed because one side remains predictable or because adverse movements are less likely to align structurally. Dual-variable systems face a broader range of synchronized downside intervals. This makes their most dangerous periods both more probable and more damaging.

The contrast shows that dual variability is not uniformly destabilizing at all moments. Its greatest intensity appears when adverse conditions synchronize. Variability synchronization risk therefore defines the interval-specific danger of simultaneous downside movement in both load and inflow.

Asymmetric variability occurs when instability is present on both sides of the system but with unequal magnitude, timing, or structural effect. Expenses may fluctuate more sharply than income, or income may fluctuate more severely than expenses. This creates imbalance patterns that differ from fully symmetric dual instability. The system is still dual-variable, but the burden is distributed unevenly across the two sides.

This mechanism defines asymmetry as unequal contribution to total instability. One side may remain moderately unstable while the other side becomes highly unstable, creating a dominant source of disruption. Even so, the presence of instability on both sides preserves the interaction problem. The system still lacks a fully reliable anchor.

Across time, asymmetric systems may appear more manageable than highly volatile systems on both sides, but they remain structurally fragile because the less unstable side still fails to provide complete stabilization. A highly variable expense profile can overwhelm moderately unstable inflow, and highly variable inflow can destabilize even moderately variable expenses. The imbalance between variable forces changes the pattern of risk but does not remove multiplicative exposure.

The contrast shows that dual variability does not require equal fluctuation to be dangerous. Systems may be asymmetrically unstable and still experience strong interaction effects. Asymmetric variability therefore defines the uneven but still compounded form of dual-variable instability.

Stability breakdown under dual variability occurs when the system loses predictable behavior because both load and inflow have become too unstable to maintain consistent alignment. At this point, pressure, reserve use, and runway compression no longer appear as isolated disruptions. They become features of the system's ongoing operation. Breakdown is defined by the collapse of predictability as much as by the rise of stress.

This mechanism defines breakdown as loss of reliable system behavior under interacting uncertainty. When one variable remains stable, the system can still organize around that anchor. Under dual variability, that anchor disappears. The result is a system in which interval outcomes become difficult to forecast and difficult to stabilize, even when average conditions appear manageable.

Across time, breakdown manifests as frequent pressure events, deeper dependence on liquidity, shorter and less stable runway, and greater sensitivity to synchronization risk. Stable systems absorb uncertainty because one side remains structurally dependable. Dual-variable systems do not have that counterweight. Small disruptions propagate faster because the system already lacks a stable balancing component.

The contrast shows that breakdown here is not merely severe stress. It is the loss of reliable operating structure under combined fluctuation. Stability breakdown under dual variability therefore defines the point at which the system ceases to behave predictably enough to sustain ordinary resilience.

Containment limits of single-sided stability refer to the fact that stabilizing only expenses or only income is not sufficient once instability is strong on the opposite side. A system with smooth expenses but highly unstable income still faces reserve stress and sequencing risk. A system with stable income but volatile expenses still faces irregular depletion and pressure. Single-sided stability contains part of the problem but not the full interaction field.

This mechanism defines containment limits as the maximum stabilizing effect of one reliable variable when the other remains unstable. One stable side can reduce volatility relative to full dual instability, but it cannot eliminate the instability generated by the moving side. Once the unstable side becomes sufficiently severe, the stable side functions as a weakened anchor rather than a full solution. The system remains exposed to recurrent pressure.

Across time, single-sided stability delays breakdown more effectively than full dual instability, but it does not fully restore predictability. Liquidity remains more necessary, runway remains more compressible, and timing risk remains active because one side still shifts unpredictably. This means the system retains partial containment, not complete resilience.

The contrast shows that stabilizing one variable is meaningful but limited. Systems with one stable side outperform systems with none, but they still operate below the stability of two-sided reliability. Containment limits of single-sided stability therefore define why one anchored component cannot fully neutralize the risks created by the other unstable component.

Multiplicative instability as system constraint means that dual variability sets an upper boundary on how much instability the system can absorb before predictable stability becomes structurally unattainable. When expense and income variability interact, the system does not merely become more difficult to manage. It enters a regime where interaction-driven amplification itself becomes a limiting condition. This is the constraint imposed by compounded uncertainty.

This mechanism defines multiplicative instability as a structural ceiling on resilience under dual-variable conditions. As interaction effects intensify, liquidity is consumed faster, runway shortens more abruptly, and pressure becomes more recurrent. These are not isolated consequences. They are interconnected outcomes of a system whose unstable parts now amplify one another. The result is a narrowing of the system's viable operating range.

Across time, systems below this constraint may still preserve functioning because variability remains bounded enough for reserves and timing structure to compensate. Systems above it lose that possibility because the interaction between unstable load and unstable inflow overwhelms single-sided containment, reserve bridging, and ordinary recovery. The constraint therefore marks the point where compounded fluctuation defines system behavior more than any individual stabilizing feature.

The contrast makes the chapter's central claim explicit. Dual variability is not simply "more instability." It is a different category of instability in which interaction creates nonlinear limits on resilience. Multiplicative instability as system constraint therefore defines the upper risk boundary of the expense-income system under combined fluctuation.

Expense Alignment with Income Structure

Alignment is defined as structural synchronization between inflow and outflow across the dimensions that determine system stability. It does not mean that income and expenses merely coexist within the same system. It means that the way expenses are applied corresponds to the way income becomes available. This establishes alignment as a coordination property rather than a simple accounting condition.

This mechanism defines alignment as a relationship between system components rather than a characteristic of either component alone. Outflow can be structurally sound on its own and still become destabilizing if it is not coordinated with inflow. In the same way, inflow can be sufficient in aggregate and still fail to stabilize the system if its structure does not match the structure of load. Alignment therefore depends on how these forces interact across time.

Across intervals, aligned systems preserve continuity because inflow and outflow move in compatible patterns. Misaligned systems experience recurring friction between demand and support, requiring buffer use and generating pressure even when totals appear manageable. The difference is not simply one of scale, but of coordination. Stable systems exhibit synchronized structure, while unstable systems exhibit structural divergence.

The contrast shows that alignment is not a decorative refinement of balance. It is a system condition that determines whether load and capacity cooperate or collide. Alignment therefore defines the coordinated structure through which inflow and outflow operate without generating avoidable instability.

Alignment differs from balance because alignment refers to synchronization, while balance refers only to aggregate equality between inflow and outflow. A system can be balanced in totals and still remain unstable if timing, magnitude, or variability are poorly coordinated. This distinction is necessary because aggregate equality does not guarantee interval-level stability. Balance is arithmetic, but alignment is structural.

This mechanism defines balance as a summary relationship and alignment as an operating relationship. Balance evaluates whether total inflow is sufficient relative to total outflow over a broad period. Alignment evaluates whether the structure of load matches the structure of support as demand is actually applied. A system can therefore appear balanced while remaining persistently exposed to pressure.

Across time, balanced-but-misaligned systems generate sequencing gaps, irregular reserve dependence, and repeated pressure events because inflow and outflow do not coordinate when it matters. Aligned systems may also be balanced, but their defining advantage is that support is available in the right pattern, not merely in the right total. This distinction becomes especially visible when variability or timing mismatch is present. Stability depends more on structural coordination than on periodic aggregate equality.

The contrast shows why balance is insufficient as a stability test. Systems that are balanced but misaligned remain fragile, while systems that are aligned reduce friction between load and support. Alignment versus balance therefore defines the difference between accounting sufficiency and operational stability.

Timing alignment occurs when expenses are applied at intervals that correspond to the availability of income. It is the sequencing dimension of synchronization, defining whether load meets support at the point of application rather than only in aggregate over time. This makes timing alignment a direct stabilizer of interval-level system behavior. When timing is aligned, pressure is less likely to emerge from ordinary demand.

This mechanism defines timing alignment as sequence compatibility between inflow and outflow. Expenses do not need to occur at identical moments as income, but they must be arranged within a structure that preserves short-term absorbability. When support arrives before or with demand, the system operates smoothly. When support arrives after demand, the system depends more heavily on liquidity or experiences direct imbalance.

Across time, aligned systems maintain predictable short-term stability because the order of events supports continuity. Misaligned systems may have sufficient total inflow and still experience recurring pressure due to sequencing gaps. This means timing alignment reduces instability without requiring lower load magnitude. The system becomes more stable not because demand is smaller, but because demand is better sequenced relative to support.

The contrast shows that sequence matters independently of total sufficiency. Systems with timing alignment preserve continuity at the interval level, while systems without it translate ordinary load into repeated pressure. Timing alignment therefore defines how sequencing supports system stability.

Timing misalignment effects emerge when expenses occur before income is available, creating sequencing gaps between load and support. These effects are structural because they arise from order, not necessarily from insufficient totals. When demand arrives before replenishment, the system must use liquidity or tolerate immediate imbalance. This makes timing misalignment a direct generator of pressure.

This mechanism defines timing misalignment as divergence in the order of inflow and outflow events. Even if total inflow eventually matches total outflow, interval-level instability appears when support is not available when load is applied. The system experiences this as reserve dependence, elevated short-term fragility, or pressure formation. Misalignment therefore changes how ordinary expenses behave inside the system.

Across time, repeated sequencing gaps create patterns of recurring reserve use and frequent interval stress. Aligned systems avoid this pattern because the order of demand and support is coordinated enough to preserve continuity. Misaligned systems, by contrast, convert routine outflow into a sequence-based instability mechanism. The result is not only more frequent pressure, but greater sensitivity to variability and shock because the system is already operating out of sequence.

The contrast shows that timing misalignment is not a minor technical imperfection. Systems with stable sequencing absorb load smoothly, while systems with unstable sequencing repeatedly bridge or breach. Timing misalignment effects therefore define how divergence in sequence becomes a structural source of instability.

Magnitude alignment occurs when the level of expense load matches the scale of inflow capacity in a way that preserves interval and multi-interval stability. It is the sizing dimension of synchronization, defining whether the system's demand level is proportionate to the income structure supporting it. This does not require static equality at every moment, but it does require that load remain compatible with the inflow base. When magnitude is aligned, support can sustain demand without chronic compression.

This mechanism defines magnitude alignment as proportional coherence between the scale of expenses and the scale of income. If load is systematically larger than inflow structure can support, the system depends excessively on liquidity and compresses runway. If load is proportionate, the system can absorb ordinary demand without persistent reserve erosion. Magnitude alignment therefore concerns structural fit, not momentary convenience.

Across time, aligned systems maintain a stable relationship between average or recurring load and the scale of replenishment. Misaligned systems do not merely spend more; they impose a demand level that the inflow structure cannot support reliably. This drives repeated pressure, slower reserve recovery, and increased fragility under variation. The instability comes from mismatch in scale, not merely from isolated intervals of excess.

The contrast shows that magnitude alignment is different from timing alignment. Sequence can be correct and still fail if the demand level overwhelms the support structure. Magnitude alignment therefore defines how proportional fit between load and inflow contributes to stable system behavior.

Magnitude misalignment emerges when the level of expense load exceeds the supporting capacity of income structure, even if timing remains coordinated. In this condition, demand is too large relative to inflow, causing recurring dependence on stored capacity or repeated pressure events. The system may be sequenced correctly and still remain unstable because the scale of load is incompatible with the scale of support. This makes magnitude misalignment a distinct source of fragility.

This mechanism defines magnitude misalignment as structural excess of load relative to inflow. The problem is not that income fails to arrive at the right time, but that even when it does arrive, it is insufficient to sustain the imposed demand pattern without reserve erosion. Misalignment in scale produces compression of liquidity, margin, and runway. It therefore weakens the system even when sequencing is orderly.

Across time, misaligned systems experience cumulative consequences because reserves must repeatedly compensate for structural excess. Aligned systems maintain proportionality and therefore preserve more consistent recovery between intervals. Misaligned systems carry too much load for the inflow base supporting them, which makes them more sensitive to variability, drift, or minor disruption. This shifts the system from stable operation into chronic stress.

The contrast shows that magnitude misalignment can destabilize an otherwise orderly structure. Systems with correct sequencing but excessive load remain fragile, while systems with proper proportionality preserve sustainability. Magnitude misalignment effects therefore define how scale divergence converts coordination into insufficiency.

Variability alignment occurs when fluctuations in expense load are structurally matched by fluctuations in inflow capacity. It is the pattern dimension of synchronization, defining whether movement on one side of the system is compatible with movement on the other. This means that the system can remain stable under fluctuation, not because variability disappears, but because variability is mirrored or absorbable across both sides. Variability alignment therefore stabilizes movement rather than eliminating it.

This mechanism defines variability alignment as compatibility between the volatility patterns of load and inflow. If expenses fluctuate upward in intervals when inflow is also structurally stronger or more available, the system can absorb those changes with limited instability. If the fluctuation patterns diverge, reserve use and pressure become more frequent. Alignment in variability is therefore not about low variance alone, but about coordinated variance.

Across time, aligned systems experience changing conditions without necessarily entering recurrent pressure, because the pattern of support remains structurally compatible with the pattern of demand. Misaligned systems experience volatility mismatch, where one side moves unpredictably relative to the other. This increases the frequency of interval breaches and the burden on liquidity. Variability alignment therefore converts fluctuation from a destabilizing pattern into a more absorbable one.

The contrast shows that variability is not inherently destabilizing if its pattern is coordinated. Systems with aligned fluctuation maintain stability under movement, while systems with unaligned fluctuation magnify instability through mismatch. Variability alignment therefore defines the synchronization of volatility across inflow and outflow.

Variability misalignment effects emerge when expense fluctuations and income fluctuations do not match in form, intensity, or timing. This creates uneven movement across the two sides of the system, increasing the likelihood that high demand coincides with weak or unstable support. The instability comes not merely from volatility itself, but from incompatible volatility patterns. This makes variability misalignment a driver of recurrent and hard-to-absorb stress.

This mechanism defines variability misalignment as divergence in how inflow and outflow fluctuate. Expenses may become irregular while income remains steady in the wrong pattern, or income may fluctuate in ways that fail to support the changing expense structure. The system then loses the capacity to absorb movement without frequent reserve bridging. Variability becomes destabilizing because it is uncoordinated.

Across time, misaligned systems produce more frequent pressure and deeper liquidity use because their periods of elevated demand are not offset by periods of elevated support. Aligned systems can tolerate more movement because fluctuation is structurally compatible. Misaligned systems face dual pressure: they absorb both volatility itself and the absence of matching support. This shortens recovery intervals and intensifies fragility.

The contrast shows that the problem is not simply "too much variability." Systems with coordinated fluctuation remain more stable, while systems with mismatched fluctuation convert variance into repeated imbalance. Variability misalignment effects therefore define how divergence in movement patterns generates structural instability.

Multi-dimensional alignment is the coordinated synchronization of timing, magnitude, and variability across inflow and outflow simultaneously. It defines a higher-order stability condition in which the system is not merely aligned on one dimension while misaligned on others. This matters because a system can have correct sequencing but improper scale, or proper scale but incompatible volatility. True structural stability requires coordination across multiple dimensions at once.

This mechanism defines multi-dimensional alignment as compound compatibility rather than isolated fit. Timing alignment reduces sequence gaps, magnitude alignment preserves proportionality, and variability alignment stabilizes movement. When all three operate together, the system experiences lower friction between demand and support. When one or more dimensions diverge, instability enters through the remaining gap.

Across time, systems with multi-dimensional alignment maintain more predictable reserve behavior, lower pressure frequency, and more stable runway trajectories. Systems with partial alignment improve relative to fully misaligned systems, but they remain exposed to the unresolved dimension. This means that single-dimension fit can moderate instability without eliminating it. Multi-dimensional alignment therefore represents a more complete coordination state.

The contrast shows that alignment is not fully captured by any one dimension alone. Systems coordinated across timing, magnitude, and variability sustain stability more robustly than systems aligned on only one axis. Multi-dimensional alignment therefore defines the structural completeness of synchronization within the expense-income system.

Alignment and pressure reduction are linked because structural synchronization reduces the frequency and severity of intervals in which load exceeds available capacity. Pressure emerges when inflow and outflow diverge in sequence, scale, or fluctuation. Alignment reduces those divergences before they convert into imbalance. This makes pressure reduction a direct consequence of coordinated system structure.

This mechanism defines pressure reduction as the stabilizing outcome of synchronized inflow and outflow. When expenses arrive in compatible sequence, at proportionate levels, and with absorbable fluctuation relative to income, fewer intervals require reserve bridging and fewer intervals breach short-term capacity. Alignment therefore acts upstream of pressure. It reduces the conditions that generate it rather than merely managing it after formation.

Across time, aligned systems exhibit fewer acute pressure events because they spend less time forcing the system to reconcile incompatible demand and support conditions. Misaligned systems do the opposite: even manageable totals generate pressure because the structure of coordination is weak. The system then relies more heavily on liquidity and becomes more sensitive to minor disturbances. Pressure becomes a recurring byproduct of divergence.

The contrast shows that pressure is not determined only by excess demand. It is also determined by lack of synchronization. Alignment and pressure reduction therefore define how coordinated structure lowers interval-level instability without requiring absolute reduction of load.

Alignment and liquidity dependence are linked because synchronization between inflow and outflow reduces the need to use stored capacity as a compensatory bridge. Liquidity exists to absorb mismatch, sequence failure, and temporary insufficiency. When alignment improves, those mismatches occur less often. The system therefore relies less on reserves to maintain ordinary continuity.

This mechanism defines reduced liquidity dependence as an outcome of structural coordination rather than reserve abundance alone. An aligned system may still hold liquidity, but it consumes it less frequently under ordinary conditions because support and demand fit together more effectively. A misaligned system uses liquidity more often, not necessarily because total resources are smaller, but because coordination is weaker. This increases reserve cycling and long-term depletion pressure.

Across time, aligned systems preserve more of their short-term absorptive capacity because ordinary demand is met more often through direct coordination with income structure. Misaligned systems repeatedly convert routine operations into reserve events. This weakens the system even when current liquidity appears sufficient, because stored capacity is being used to compensate for preventable divergence. Reserve dependence therefore becomes a sign of coordination failure rather than simply of low resources.

The contrast shows that liquidity is buffer, not alignment itself. Systems that are aligned require less compensation, while systems that are misaligned rely more heavily on compensation. Alignment and liquidity dependence therefore define how synchronization reduces the burden placed on stored capacity.

Alignment and runway stability are linked because coordinated inflow and outflow produce more consistent reserve use, which in turn stabilizes the system's time-to-failure profile. Runway is shaped by how quickly liquidity is consumed relative to replenishment. Alignment slows avoidable drawdown by reducing structural mismatch. This makes runway not only longer in some cases, but more predictable across time.

This mechanism defines runway stability as consistency in survival duration under ongoing system operation. When timing, magnitude, and variability are better synchronized, depletion occurs in a more orderly pattern. The system does not experience frequent abrupt compressions from preventable mismatches. Misalignment, by contrast, causes runway to shorten unpredictably through repeated reserve drains and irregular support failures.

Across time, aligned systems maintain more stable projections of remaining duration because consumption and replenishment interact in a coordinated way. Misaligned systems see runway fluctuate or compress sharply, even when average totals do not appear severe. The loss is not only of time, but of temporal reliability. This matters because unstable runway behavior reflects deeper structural instability in reserve use.

The contrast shows that runway depends on more than reserve quantity. It depends on whether inflow and outflow are coordinated enough to preserve reserves efficiently. Alignment and runway stability therefore define how synchronization supports a steadier time horizon under ongoing demand.

Alignment under variability refers to the system's ability to preserve synchronization even when both load and inflow move across intervals rather than remaining fixed. This is a more demanding condition than alignment under static circumstances because fluctuation must remain coordinated rather than merely low. The question is not whether variation exists, but whether the variation is structurally absorbable. This makes alignment under variability a higher-order test of system resilience.

This mechanism defines variable-state alignment as maintained correspondence across changing conditions. Expenses may fluctuate and income may fluctuate, but if their movement remains compatible in timing, scale, and pattern, the system can remain stable. This differs from systems where variability itself creates divergence. Under those conditions, each fluctuation widens mismatch rather than preserving structure.

Across time, systems that maintain alignment under variability experience movement without repeated breakdown in coordination. Reserve use remains more controlled, pressure forms less often, and runway degrades less erratically. Systems that lose alignment under variability become increasingly dependent on liquidity because every fluctuation becomes a destabilizing event rather than a compatible adjustment. The instability lies in the loss of synchronization, not in fluctuation alone.

The contrast shows that variability does not automatically eliminate alignment. Systems can remain coordinated under movement if that movement is structurally matched. Alignment under variability therefore defines the capacity of a system to remain synchronized through changing rather than static conditions.

Misalignment is an instability driver because divergence between inflow and outflow across timing, magnitude, or variability generates the conditions under which pressure, reserve dependence, and stress emerge. The system becomes unstable not only when load is large, but when load and support are poorly coordinated. Misalignment therefore acts as a structural source of instability independent of simple totals. It is the mechanism through which manageable components become destabilizing when arranged incompatibly.

This mechanism defines misalignment as divergence in operating structure. Timing misalignment creates sequence gaps, magnitude misalignment creates unsupported scale, and variability misalignment creates uncoordinated movement. Each form increases the burden on liquidity and shortens the distance to pressure. When multiple forms occur together, instability intensifies because divergence compounds.

Across time, misaligned systems convert ordinary functioning into repeated stress. Instead of demand and support operating as coordinated elements, they operate as competing forces that must be reconciled after the fact. This increases reserve cycling, reduces predictability, and raises pressure frequency. The system loses stability not because one component is necessarily extreme, but because the relationship between components is dysfunctional.

The contrast shows that instability is often relational rather than purely scalar. Systems with aligned structure remain stable under conditions that misaligned systems cannot tolerate. Misalignment as instability driver therefore defines how divergence in system coordination produces recurring structural fragility.

Alignment as a structural stability mechanism means that coordinated inflow and outflow reduce avoidable mismatch across the dimensions that generate pressure. Stability emerges not merely from lower load or higher income, but from the synchronized relationship between them. This makes alignment a mechanism of organization rather than one of simple reduction. Its stabilizing force lies in coordination.

This mechanism defines alignment as a system property that lowers friction between demand and support. Timing alignment reduces sequencing failure, magnitude alignment reduces unsupported scale, and variability alignment reduces incompatible movement. Together these forms of coordination reduce pressure frequency, preserve liquidity, and stabilize runway behavior. Alignment therefore improves system performance by reducing structural inefficiency in how load meets capacity.

Across time, aligned systems maintain more predictable and less reserve-intensive operation because inflow and outflow cooperate rather than collide. Misaligned systems may survive through compensation, but they do so with higher liquidity dependence, more frequent pressure, and greater fragility. The difference is not that one system always has less load, but that one system organizes load more compatibly relative to income structure. Stability becomes a property of coordinated architecture rather than reactive correction.

The contrast makes the chapter's central point explicit. Alignment is not equality, and it is not behavioral adjustment. It is structural synchronization across the operating dimensions of the system. Alignment as a structural stability mechanism therefore defines why coordinated architecture reduces instability without requiring the elimination of load.

Expense Rigidity vs. Flexibility

Rigidity is defined as load that cannot be adjusted when system conditions change. It represents the portion of expense structure that remains fixed in timing, magnitude, or presence even when inflow weakens, liquidity declines, or pressure rises. This makes rigidity a structural property of load rather than a temporary condition of inconvenience. Within the expense system, rigidity limits the ability to respond to changing capacity.

This mechanism defines rigid load as non-adjustable demand embedded in the operating structure. When conditions deteriorate, rigid expenses continue to apply force at the same level or in the same pattern, regardless of whether support remains adequate. The issue is not merely that the load exists, but that the system has no internal means of reconfiguring it. Rigidity therefore converts changing external conditions into unavoidable internal stress.

Across time, rigid systems accumulate fragility because each interval of changing capacity must be absorbed without corresponding adjustment in load. Stable systems may contain some rigid load, but not at a level that overwhelms adjustment capacity elsewhere in the system. Highly rigid systems do the opposite: they force continuity of demand under conditions that no longer support it. This increases reliance on liquidity, accelerates pressure formation, and reduces recovery flexibility.

The contrast shows that rigidity is not simply a synonym for baseline. A system may have persistent load and still retain meaningful adjustability in other layers. Rigidity therefore defines the non-adjustable character of load under changing conditions.

Flexibility is defined as adjustable load under changing system conditions. It refers to the system's ability to alter expense timing, magnitude, or presence without requiring a full collapse of operating structure. This makes flexibility a structural property of adjustability rather than a behavioral act of restraint. Within the system model, flexibility creates room for adaptation before pressure becomes breakdown.

This mechanism defines flexible load as demand that can be shifted, resized, delayed, or removed as support conditions change. Flexibility does not eliminate expenses altogether; it changes how tightly those expenses are bound to a fixed pattern. A flexible system can reduce mismatch between load and capacity by modifying the form of demand rather than absorbing it unchanged. This gives the system internal degrees of freedom under stress.

Across time, flexible systems preserve stability more effectively because they can alter load before or as conditions worsen. When inflow weakens or variability rises, flexible load can be reconfigured in ways that reduce the need for reserve use. Rigid systems lack this capacity and must absorb disruption through liquidity depletion or direct pressure. Flexibility therefore changes how the system experiences adverse conditions.

The contrast shows that flexibility is not the absence of load but the presence of adjustment capacity. Systems with flexible load remain more adaptive under uncertainty, while systems without it remain exposed to fixed demand patterns. Flexibility therefore defines the adjustability layer of system stability.

Rigidity versus flexibility is the structural contrast between non-adjustable load and adjustable load within the expense system. Rigidity fixes demand into patterns that persist regardless of changing support conditions, while flexibility allows those patterns to be altered in response to system movement. This distinction determines whether the system absorbs change through reconfiguration or through pressure. It is therefore a core contrast in how load behaves under constraint.

This mechanism defines rigidity and flexibility not as opposites in abstract terms, but as competing structural properties of expense design. Rigid load imposes continuity of demand even when inflow, liquidity, or margin deteriorate. Flexible load allows the system to alter demand shape before instability deepens. The difference is not about whether expenses exist, but about whether the system can modify their operation.

Across time, systems with higher rigidity display repeated dependence on reserves and more rapid pressure escalation under change. Systems with higher flexibility display better preservation of alignment because they can adjust load before mismatch becomes acute. Both systems may face the same external disturbance, but their internal response profiles differ. One must absorb without adaptation; the other can adapt before absorption fails.

The contrast shows why this distinction matters beyond descriptive classification. Rigidity amplifies fragility under changing conditions, while flexibility increases tolerance to change. Rigidity versus flexibility therefore defines whether the expense system is structurally exposed or structurally adaptive.

Sources of rigidity are the structural features that make expenses non-adjustable once they are embedded in the system. These sources determine why certain forms of load remain fixed under changing conditions rather than being modifiable in timing, magnitude, or presence. Rigidity does not appear randomly; it is produced by the way obligations are configured. This makes its causes architectural rather than incidental.

This mechanism defines rigidity sources as embedded conditions that lock demand into place. These may include persistent obligations, synchronized payment requirements, fixed service dependencies, or structures that tie operation to a specific minimum level of expense. What matters is not the label of the expense but the inability to alter it when support deteriorates. The source of rigidity is therefore the structural design that makes adjustment unavailable.

Across time, systems with many rigidity sources become increasingly exposed to instability because adverse changes on the capacity side cannot be met with corresponding demand changes. A decline in inflow, an increase in variability, or a liquidity drawdown produces more stress when the expense structure contains many non-adjustable elements. Systems with fewer rigidity sources retain more internal room to respond. This creates a widening divergence in resilience under change.

The contrast shows that rigidity is not merely a property of "high expenses." It is a property of how tightly expenses are locked into the system. Sources of rigidity therefore define the structural origins of non-adjustable load.

Sources of flexibility are the structural conditions that allow load to be adjusted when the system encounters change. These conditions determine whether expenses can be shifted, reduced, paused, or reconfigured without disabling the system's core operation. Flexibility therefore arises from design features that preserve optionality inside the expense structure. It is not spontaneous responsiveness, but embedded adjustability.

This mechanism defines flexibility sources as features of load architecture that permit change without immediate system failure. These may include variable timing, scalable magnitude, optional components, or arrangements in which demand is not fully synchronized into rigid commitments. What matters is that the structure allows modification when capacity changes. The system is therefore not forced to carry every expense in an unchanged form across all conditions.

Across time, systems with multiple flexibility sources absorb disruption more effectively because they possess internal means of reducing mismatch. When inflow weakens or variability rises, these systems can reconfigure load without relying exclusively on liquidity. Systems without such sources cannot alter demand structure and must absorb stress through reserves or direct instability. This difference accumulates as conditions become more volatile.

The contrast shows that flexibility is not a matter of having fewer expenses in general. It is a matter of having structural room to modify expense behavior. Sources of flexibility therefore define the architectural basis of system adaptability.

Rigidity and pressure formation are linked because non-adjustable load continues to apply force even when the system's capacity to absorb it has weakened. When inflow declines, timing shifts, or liquidity thins, rigid demand remains unchanged and therefore converts external change into direct imbalance. This makes rigidity a pressure amplifier under changing conditions. The inability to adjust becomes the mechanism that turns changing conditions into recurring pressure.

This mechanism defines rigid pressure formation as mismatch produced by fixed demand under variable support. If expenses could be altered, some of that mismatch could be reduced before capacity is breached. But when demand remains fixed, each deterioration on the support side increases the likelihood that load will exceed available capacity. Rigidity therefore narrows the system's response options and moves instability closer to the surface.

Across time, rigid systems experience more frequent pressure because every disturbance must be absorbed without the benefit of load reconfiguration. Flexible systems may still face disruption, but they can reduce or reshape demand to preserve alignment. Rigid systems cannot do so, which increases the frequency, depth, and persistence of imbalance. The problem is not just that pressure occurs, but that the system has fewer internal ways to prevent it from recurring.

The contrast shows that pressure is not only a function of excessive load. It is also a function of non-adjustable load under changing support.

Rigidity and pressure formation therefore define how inflexibility turns changing conditions into immediate structural stress.

Flexibility as a load adjustment mechanism means that the system can alter demand in response to changing inflow, liquidity, or timing conditions before those changes become acute instability. This makes flexibility an active stabilizer of the load side of the system. It does not remove the existence of expenses, but it changes how those expenses behave under stress. Flexibility therefore operates as an internal mechanism for preserving alignment.

This mechanism defines adjustment as the ability to modify load in timing, magnitude, or presence when conditions shift. By doing so, the system reduces the probability that a change in support will translate directly into pressure. Flexible load creates more response pathways than rigid load because it can be reshaped instead of simply endured. This gives the system a structural way to reduce mismatch before reserves are exhausted.

Across time, systems with flexible adjustment capacity preserve stability more effectively because they do not force all change to be absorbed by liquidity. When inflow weakens or variability increases, these systems can reduce the rate at which stress accumulates by reconfiguring demand. Rigid systems lack this layer of response and must bridge the difference with stored capacity or direct contraction of stability. The long-term consequence is greater divergence in reserve preservation and runway durability.

The contrast shows that flexibility is not passive slack. It is a mechanism through which the system transforms adverse conditions into manageable adjustments rather than forced pressure. Flexibility as a load adjustment mechanism therefore defines how adaptable demand reduces structural instability.

Adaptability is the system's ability to reconfigure load in response to changing conditions without collapsing its operating structure. It is broader than flexibility in any one expense category because it describes the system-level capacity to respond through coordinated adjustment. This makes adaptability the response property that emerges from the presence of flexible load within the overall expense architecture. A system can only adapt if its structure allows change to occur.

This mechanism defines adaptability as operational response capacity under altered inflow, reserve, timing, or variability conditions. Flexibility provides the adjustable elements, but adaptability describes the system's ability to use those elements in a coordinated way to preserve stability. Rigid systems may contain isolated flexible elements and still remain poorly adaptable if their overall structure prevents meaningful reconfiguration. Adaptability therefore depends on how deeply flexibility exists across the system.

Across time, adaptable systems maintain continuity under disruption because they can reshape demand fast enough to avoid repeated structural breach. Non-adaptable systems do not necessarily fail immediately, but they absorb each disruption with less room to respond and therefore accumulate stress more rapidly. This changes the long-term survival profile of the system. Adaptability preserves resilience not by eliminating change, but by giving the system a way to respond structurally to change.

The contrast shows that flexibility at the expense level and adaptability at the system level are related but distinct. Flexibility is the adjustable property of load; adaptability is the coordinated response capacity built from it. Adaptability as system response therefore defines how the expense system behaves under changing conditions.

Rigidity under income disruption refers to the effect of non-adjustable load when inflow declines, delays, or becomes unreliable. Because rigid expenses do not change with reduced support, the system must absorb the full impact of income disruption through liquidity depletion or direct pressure. This makes income instability much more damaging in rigid structures than in adaptable ones. The load remains constant while support weakens.

This mechanism defines rigid income-response failure as the absence of demand-side adjustment during inflow deterioration. In a system with rigid load, reduced income does not trigger structural reduction in demand. Instead, the gap must be bridged through reserves, which accelerates depletion and shortens runway. If reserves are insufficient, pressure appears more quickly because demand continues unchanged under weaker support.

Across time, rigid systems under income disruption exhibit faster deterioration because each interval of reduced inflow occurs against the same fixed expense structure. Flexible systems also experience stress under income disruption, but they can change the expense profile enough to reduce the gap. Rigid systems cannot do so, which means that inflow disruption is converted directly into reserve consumption and fragility. This makes them especially vulnerable under uncertain or declining income.

The contrast shows that income disruption is not experienced equally across all systems. Where load is rigid, inflow decline becomes much harder to contain. Rigidity under income disruption therefore defines how non-adjustable demand amplifies instability when support weakens.

Flexibility under income disruption refers to the system's ability to adjust load when inflow declines, delays, or becomes unstable. Because flexible expenses can be reconfigured, the system can reduce the mismatch between support and demand before reserves are fully relied upon. This does not eliminate disruption, but it changes how disruption is absorbed. Flexibility therefore functions as a stabilizing response under weakened inflow.

This mechanism defines flexible income response as demand-side adaptation to changes in support. When income falls or becomes irregular, flexible systems alter expense timing, scale, or presence to preserve alignment more effectively. This lowers the amount of shortfall that must be covered by liquidity. In structural terms, flexibility acts as a substitute for some of the stability that declining inflow has removed.

Across time, systems with flexible load preserve more continuity under income disruption because they consume reserves more slowly and maintain longer runway. Rigid systems facing the same disruption bridge the entire gap with liquidity, which accelerates depletion. Flexible systems therefore delay or reduce the transition from inflow weakness to pressure and stress. Their advantage is not immunity to disruption, but response capacity within disruption.

The contrast shows that reduced inflow does not automatically create the same outcome in every structure. Systems with flexibility can partially absorb disruption through reconfiguration, while systems without it must absorb disruption through reserve loss. Flexibility under income disruption therefore defines how adjustable load supports stability when inflow weakens.

Rigidity and runway compression are linked because non-adjustable load maintains a high rate of reserve consumption even when support conditions deteriorate. Runway is determined by how long liquidity can sustain current demand. When demand cannot be reduced, depletion continues at an unchanged or insufficiently reduced pace, which shortens time-to-failure. Rigidity therefore compresses runway by locking the depletion rate in place.

This mechanism defines rigid runway compression as accelerated loss of survival duration under fixed load. If inflow weakens, variability rises, or shock occurs, a flexible system may slow reserve consumption through load adjustment. A rigid system cannot do so, meaning the reserve burn rate remains high relative to available support. This converts changing conditions into faster loss of remaining time.

Across time, rigid systems show steeper declines in runway because every disruption is met with unchanged demand and therefore stronger reserve drain. Flexible systems preserve more duration because they can reduce the load acting on reserves. The difference accumulates quickly under prolonged stress. A rigid structure therefore not only reduces current resilience but weakens future survival duration more aggressively.

The contrast shows that runway is not shaped by reserves alone. It is also shaped by whether load can be modified as those reserves come under pressure. Rigidity and runway compression therefore define how inflexibility shortens the system's remaining operating horizon.

Flexibility and runway preservation are linked because adjustable load allows the system to reduce reserve consumption when support weakens or uncertainty rises. Since runway measures the duration reserves can sustain demand, any mechanism that slows depletion helps preserve remaining time. Flexibility does this by changing the expense burden applied to liquidity. It therefore acts as a structural protector of time-to-failure.

This mechanism defines runway preservation as the extension or stabilization of survival duration through reduced demand on reserves. When expenses can be adjusted, the system lowers the rate at which liquidity is consumed during adverse periods. This does not create new reserves, but it allows existing reserves to last longer. Flexibility therefore affects runway through the depletion side of the equation.

Across time, flexible systems maintain more stable and longer runway under changing conditions because they can reduce mismatch before reserve use becomes extreme. Rigid systems facing the same disruption lose runway more quickly because demand remains fixed while support deteriorates. The divergence becomes especially important during prolonged inflow weakness or repeated variability. Flexible structures preserve time by moderating load.

The contrast shows that runway preservation is not only a liquidity problem. It is also a load-adjustability problem. Flexibility and runway preservation therefore define how adaptable demand sustains the temporal resilience of the system.

Rigidity under variability and shock refers to the way non-adjustable load amplifies instability when the system is exposed to fluctuating conditions or sudden disruptions. Variability increases the frequency of changing support or changing load patterns, while shock creates abrupt stress. In both cases, rigidity prevents the system from responding by altering demand. This forces the full burden of disruption onto liquidity and margin.

This mechanism defines rigid exposure as unchanged load under changing conditions. Under variability, repeated fluctuations create many intervals in which adjustment would reduce mismatch, but rigid systems cannot perform that adjustment. Under shock, a sudden disturbance compresses reserves or inflow support rapidly, and rigid demand continues unchanged. This turns adaptable disturbances into forced stress events.

Across time, rigid systems accumulate more pressure and reserve depletion under variability because each fluctuation must be bridged rather than partially neutralized. Under shock, they also experience sharper instability because no structural reduction in demand occurs after the event. Flexible systems still face these disturbances, but they can reduce the system's exposure through reconfiguration. Rigid systems instead magnify the effect of each disturbance through non-response.

The contrast shows that variability and shock become more dangerous when load cannot move with conditions. Systems with flexibility absorb changing states more effectively, while rigid systems translate change into accelerated fragility. Rigidity under variability and shock therefore defines how inflexibility amplifies instability under adverse movement.

Flexibility as stability buffer means that adjustable load provides a protective layer against pressure by allowing the system to reduce mismatch before it becomes acute. While liquidity buffers instability by absorbing it after it appears, flexibility buffers instability by changing the demand structure that would otherwise create it. This gives the system a preventive response layer on the load side. Flexibility therefore acts as a structural stabilizer before reserves are fully called upon.

This mechanism defines the flexibility buffer as adjustment capacity that stands between changing conditions and full structural breach. When inflow weakens, variability rises, or timing diverges, flexible load can absorb part of the change through reconfiguration. This reduces how much of the disturbance must be bridged through liquidity or suffered as direct pressure. In this sense, flexibility buffers by reducing the force of the mismatch itself.

Across time, systems with a meaningful flexibility buffer preserve liquidity longer, experience fewer repeated pressure events, and maintain a more stable runway trajectory. Systems without that buffer rely more heavily on stored capacity and therefore consume reserves more quickly. The result is not only greater current fragility but lower future resilience. Flexibility changes the system's capacity to remain stable under movement.

The contrast shows that flexibility is not merely one more optional quality of load. It is a stabilizing layer that reduces the severity of adverse conditions before they fully transmit into imbalance. Flexibility as stability buffer therefore defines how adjustable demand protects the system from escalating stress.

Adaptability as structural stability requirement means that long-term stability depends on the system's ability to reconfigure load as conditions change. A system that cannot adapt may remain stable only under narrow and static conditions. Once inflow, variability, timing, or reserves change materially, rigidity converts those changes into pressure and depletion. Adaptability is therefore not an optional enhancement of stability but a requirement for sustaining stability through time.

This mechanism defines structural adaptability as the load-side capacity to respond without collapse under shifting support conditions. Stability in a dynamic environment requires more than balance at a single point; it requires a structure that can remain viable when conditions move.

Flexibility supplies the adjustable components, and adaptability organizes those components into a meaningful response capacity. Without this, the system's stability is brittle rather than resilient.

Across time, adaptable systems maintain operation through disturbance because they can reshape demand before instability compounds. Non-adaptable systems may appear stable in calm conditions, but that stability decays quickly once uncertainty increases. They lose reserves faster, compress runway more rapidly, and experience more frequent pressure because demand cannot evolve with conditions. This makes long-term stability impossible without some structural degree of load flexibility.

The contrast makes the chapter's core claim explicit. Rigid systems can survive only while conditions remain favorable enough to support fixed demand. Flexible systems sustain stability across a wider range of conditions because they can adapt demand structurally. Adaptability as structural stability requirement therefore defines why long-term stability depends on flexible load.

Maintaining Stability Under Stress

Stress is defined as accumulated pressure across time within the expense system. It is not the same as a single interval of imbalance, but the structural burden created when repeated pressure events remain unresolved or are only partially absorbed. This makes stress a temporal condition rather than an isolated event. Within the system model, stress reflects the ongoing burden imposed by load-capacity friction that persists beyond immediate intervals.

This mechanism defines stress as the cumulative consequence of recurring mismatch between expenses and available absorptive capacity. Pressure may appear at one point and dissipate, but stress develops when those pressure events recur, compound, or leave the system weaker in subsequent intervals. Stress therefore changes the system's condition, not just its momentary state. It becomes embedded in the structure through reserve depletion, reduced tolerance, and increased sensitivity.

Across time, resilient systems may experience pressure without converting it into enduring stress because absorptive mechanisms restore stability before stress compounds. Fragile systems do the opposite: each new imbalance is layered onto unresolved stress from prior intervals. This creates a progressively weaker operating condition even if no single interval appears catastrophic. Stress is therefore the system-level record of unresolved pressure.

The contrast shows that stress cannot be understood as a larger version of pressure. Pressure is immediate imbalance; stress is the structural accumulation of that imbalance across time. Defining stress in the expense system therefore establishes the foundation for analyzing resilience under sustained stress.

Resilience is defined as the system's ability to absorb stress without losing functional stability. It describes whether the expense structure can remain operational under disruption without crossing into breakdown. This makes resilience a structural property of design rather than a reaction to difficulty after it appears. Within the system model, resilience determines whether stress is contained or amplified.

This mechanism defines resilience as absorptive endurance under cumulative pressure. A resilient system does not avoid all disturbance; it preserves function despite the presence of disturbance. That preservation depends on structural features already embedded in the system, including liquidity, alignment, flexibility, and constraint. Resilience is therefore not what the system improvises, but what its design already allows.

Across time, resilient systems may bend under pressure without collapsing into instability because they retain buffer, adjustment capacity, and coordinated structure under stress. Fragile systems may appear stable under ordinary conditions yet lose function quickly once stress begins to accumulate. The difference lies in whether prior architecture can absorb disruption without turning each pressure event into escalating system weakness. Resilience is therefore measured under stress, not in its absence.

The contrast shows that resilience is not the absence of stress but the capacity to withstand stress without failure. Systems that absorb stress preserve continuity, while systems that cannot absorb it move toward breakdown. Defining resilience therefore clarifies the chapter's core concept: stability under stress is a property of structure.

Stress differs from pressure because stress is accumulated across intervals, while pressure is a point-in-time imbalance between load and capacity.

Pressure appears when demand exceeds what the system can absorb at a particular moment. Stress appears when such events repeat, persist, or leave unresolved burden behind. This distinction is necessary because the system behaves differently under acute imbalance than under accumulated stress.

This mechanism defines pressure as interval-specific and stress as cross-interval. Pressure may be sharp but temporary, especially if reserves, timing support, or adjustment capacity absorb it quickly. Stress emerges when that same pressure is not fully resolved and instead weakens the system's future condition. Stress therefore is not merely repeated pressure; it is the structural consequence of pressure that has accumulated.

Across time, resilient systems reduce the conversion of pressure into stress by containing imbalance before it compounds. Fragile systems allow repeated pressure events to leave residue in the form of depleted liquidity, shortened runway, misalignment, or increased sensitivity. This means that the same pressure event can have different long-term effects depending on the resilience of the system that experiences it. Stress is therefore a deeper indicator of system instability than pressure alone.

The contrast shows why the two concepts must remain separate. Pressure describes immediate breach, while stress describes what repeated breach does to system condition over time. Stress versus pressure therefore defines the difference between acute imbalance and cumulative structural stress.

Structural stability under stress is the persistence of system function despite ongoing disruption or accumulated stress. It refers to whether the expense system continues to operate within viable limits even when pressure is present or conditions deteriorate. This makes structural stability a durability property of the system under adverse conditions. It is not the absence of difficulty, but the preservation of function during difficulty.

This mechanism defines stability under stress as continuity of operation without crossing failure thresholds. A structurally stable system may draw on liquidity, compress margin, or adjust load, but it retains enough coherence to prevent cascading breakdown. Structural instability appears when the same stress conditions cause reserve exhaustion, persistent misalignment, or loss of functional tolerance. The difference lies in design capacity, not in the existence of stress itself.

Across time, resilient systems preserve core function because their architecture distributes stress through multiple stabilizing layers rather than forcing it into a single failure point. Fragile systems lack this distribution and therefore concentrate stress into pressure amplification, reserve depletion, or loss of runway. Stability under stress is revealed by whether the system's core structure remains viable as conditions worsen. This makes adverse periods the real test of system design.

The contrast shows that a system can appear stable under normal conditions while lacking structural stability under stress. Systems that retain function under stress are resilient; systems that fail once stress accumulates are merely conditionally stable. Structural stability under stress therefore defines persistence of function as the measure of resilience.

Stress absorption capacity is the system's ability to contain accumulated pressure without crossing into failure. It defines how much stress the expense structure can absorb before its core functioning begins to degrade beyond recovery. This makes stress absorption a threshold property rather than a vague quality of toughness. Within the system, it reflects the combined effect of reserves, flexibility, alignment, and bounded load.

This mechanism defines absorption capacity as the amount of cumulative stress the system can carry while still maintaining viable operation. It is not identical to liquidity, runway, or margin, though all of those contribute to it. Absorption capacity describes the broader ability of the system to remain coherent while under repeated pressure. It therefore captures tolerance to persistence, not just response to isolated events.

Across time, resilient systems absorb stress through layered mechanisms that prevent each pressure event from becoming a structural break. Fragile systems have low absorption capacity, so repeated stress quickly reduces function and moves them toward threshold breach. This means two systems may face similar disruptions and yet diverge sharply based on how much stress they can contain before destabilizing. Stress absorption is therefore a differentiating property of design quality.

The contrast shows that the presence of pressure does not determine outcome by itself. The system's capacity to absorb accumulated pressure is what determines whether stress remains survivable or becomes active breakdown. Stress absorption capacity therefore defines the system's tolerance boundary under ongoing disruption.

Controlled expense structures under stress are expense systems whose load remains bounded, organized, and non-amplifying when conditions deteriorate. These structures do not eliminate pressure, but they prevent pressure from expanding through uncontrolled pathways, excessive variability, or open-ended demand. This makes control a stabilizing property during stress rather than only before stress appears. Under stress, controlled structures preserve order in how load behaves.

This mechanism defines controlled expense structure as one in which boundaries remain operative under disruption. Load does not escalate through feedback, drift, or unrestricted variability at the same time that capacity is weakening. Instead, the system retains enough structure that demand continues to behave within constrained ranges. This prevents stress from spreading through the expense side faster than absorptive mechanisms can contain it.

Across time, resilient systems retain controlled load patterns even while under pressure, which allows liquidity, runway, and flexibility to function effectively. Fragile systems lose that control under stress, causing expenses to become more destabilizing precisely when support is weakest. This compounds the burden on every other stabilizing mechanism. A controlled structure therefore increases the probability that stress remains containable rather than self-amplifying.

The contrast shows that stress response depends not only on reserves, but on whether load remains structured while reserves are being used. Controlled expense structures under stress therefore define how load design affects resilience during disruption.

System behavior under increasing stress is the progressive shift from contained stress to unstable operation as accumulated pressure grows. This behavior is not binary; the system does not move from full stability to full failure in a single step. Instead, it transitions through stages of reduced buffer, increased reserve dependence, and narrowing tolerance. This makes increasing stress a process of structural degradation.

This mechanism defines escalating stress behavior as gradual reduction in the system's ability to absorb additional stress. At lower levels of stress, stabilizing mechanisms may still operate effectively, and function remains mostly intact. As stress increases, those mechanisms begin to weaken: liquidity becomes thinner, runway shortens, flexibility is used up, and alignment becomes harder to preserve. The system therefore behaves differently at different levels of stress.

Across time, resilient systems show slower degradation because prior structure spreads stress and preserves more of the mechanisms that support continuity. Fragile systems degrade rapidly because each new interval of stress arrives against a system already weakened by earlier stress. This creates threshold migration: the level of disruption needed to cause breakdown becomes lower over time. System behavior under increasing stress therefore reveals whether resilience is durable or quickly exhausted.

The contrast shows that the important difference is not whether stress exists, but how the system evolves as stress accumulates. System behavior under increasing stress therefore defines the transition path from manageable stress to instability.

Failure threshold occurs when the expense system can no longer absorb load without losing functional stability. It is the point at which accumulated stress has reduced reserves, tolerance, coordination, or adjustment capacity enough that continued operation within existing structure is no longer viable. This makes failure threshold a structural boundary rather than an emotional or discretionary event. It marks the end of absorptive resilience.

This mechanism defines the threshold as the limit of containment. Before the threshold, pressure may be severe, but the system still retains enough function to absorb, adapt, or bridge. Beyond the threshold, additional load no longer produces contained stress; it produces breakdown in continuity. The threshold is therefore not identical to the first appearance of stress. It is the point at which stress can no longer be contained within system design.

Across time, resilient systems maintain greater distance from this threshold because stress absorption remains intact longer. Fragile systems approach it quickly because each period of pressure degrades the mechanisms that would otherwise preserve stability. This means threshold proximity itself becomes a measure of fragility. As the system weakens, smaller disturbances are required to push it across the failure boundary.

The contrast shows that failure threshold is not a dramatic external event imposed from outside. It is the structural point where design can no longer contain ongoing load. Failure threshold therefore defines the boundary between stressed continuity and functional breakdown.

Resilient versus fragile systems is the structural contrast between expense architectures that absorb stress and those that convert stress into accelerated instability. Both types may encounter similar disruption, but their internal response profiles differ because one contains stress while the other amplifies it. This makes resilience and fragility relational properties of system design under pressure. The difference appears most clearly when the system is forced away from ordinary conditions.

This mechanism defines resilient systems as structures with sufficient absorptive depth, coordinated design, and adaptive response capacity to preserve function under stress. Fragile systems, by contrast, rely on conditions remaining favorable because they lack enough buffer, flexibility, or synchronization to absorb sustained pressure. The issue is not whether either system experiences stress, but what happens after stress begins. One distributes stress; the other concentrates it.

Across time, resilient systems maintain continuity longer because reserves, runway, flexibility, and alignment continue functioning under pressure. Fragile systems lose those functions more quickly, causing stress to convert into pressure amplification, reserve exhaustion, and threshold approach. This means the same disturbance produces different trajectories depending on the underlying architecture. Resilience lengthens survivability; fragility shortens it.

The contrast shows that resilience is not a matter of intensity alone, but of response structure. Resilient versus fragile systems therefore defines how different expense architectures behave once stress becomes unavoidable.

Role of liquidity under stress is the function of buffer capacity in absorbing accumulated pressure before that pressure converts into failure. Liquidity does not eliminate stress, but it provides immediate absorptive capacity that slows or prevents the translation of pressure into structural breakdown. This makes liquidity a short-term stabilizer under adverse conditions. Under stress, it functions as the resource layer that keeps continuity viable.

This mechanism defines liquidity under stress as reserve absorption during periods when inflow is insufficient or timing misalignment intensifies. When load continues under weakened support, liquidity allows the system to maintain operation without immediate collapse. This buys time for other stabilizing mechanisms to remain operative. Without it, stress reaches failure thresholds more quickly because no reserve layer stands between pressure and breakdown.

Across time, resilient systems preserve liquidity more effectively before stress arrives and consume it more strategically while stress is active. Fragile systems often enter stress with thinner reserves and deplete them more rapidly because demand is less adjustable and more poorly aligned. This means the same stress period has very different consequences depending on reserve depth and structure. Liquidity therefore acts not just as a resource, but as a rate-limiter on instability progression.

The contrast shows that liquidity is not resilience by itself, but it is one of resilience's most immediate operating components. Role of liquidity under stress therefore defines how stored capacity buffers the system during accumulated stress.

Role of runway under stress is the temporal function of remaining survival duration while the system is under ongoing stress. If liquidity is the stock of short-term capacity, runway is the time expression of how long that stock can continue supporting the system under current conditions. This makes runway the duration layer of resilience. Under stress, it measures how long containment can continue before failure threshold is reached.

This mechanism defines runway under stress as time-based tolerance to accumulated pressure. Stress does not only consume reserves; it consumes time remaining before those reserves are exhausted. A system with longer runway can sustain stress longer without immediate collapse, giving more room for absorption and adaptation. A system with short runway experiences stress as immediate deadline pressure because reserve duration is already limited.

Across time, resilient systems preserve runway by maintaining lower reserve burn rates, better alignment, and more adjustable load under stress. Fragile systems compress runway rapidly because each interval of stress consumes reserves against a less adaptable demand profile. This makes time-to-failure shorten not just through outflow, but through the inability to moderate outflow under stress. Runway therefore reveals how quickly a stressed system is approaching structural breakdown.

The contrast shows that two systems can experience similar pressure but have very different tolerances depending on remaining duration. Role of runway under stress therefore defines the temporal boundary of resilience under accumulated stress.

Role of flexibility under stress is the adjustment capacity that allows the system to modify load as pressure accumulates, thereby reducing the direct burden on liquidity and runway. Flexibility does not remove stress already present, but it changes how much additional stress must be absorbed in unchanged form. This makes flexibility the adaptive component of resilience under stress. Where flexibility exists, the system can respond structurally before pressure fully hardens into breakdown.

This mechanism defines flexibility under stress as demand-side adjustability during active stress. When inflow declines, variability rises, or reserves thin, flexible load can be reconfigured in timing, scale, or presence. This reduces mismatch and slows the rate at which stress compounds. Systems without flexibility cannot perform this adjustment and therefore force reserves to absorb a larger share of pressure.

Across time, resilient systems use flexibility to preserve function by reducing how much of each new disturbance must be borne by stored capacity alone. Fragile systems lack this option and experience faster reserve exhaustion, shorter runway, and quicker threshold approach under the same stress sequence. Flexibility therefore spreads stress away from a single pressure channel. It makes the system's stress response more distributed and less brittle.

The contrast shows that flexibility is not merely useful during calm conditions. Its importance becomes greatest when support deteriorates and the system must adapt to survive. Role of flexibility under stress therefore defines how adjustable load contributes to resilience under accumulated pressure.

Role of alignment under stress is the preservation of synchronization between inflow and outflow when conditions are disrupted. Alignment reduces the number of unnecessary mismatches that would otherwise convert already existing stress into additional pressure. This makes alignment a coordination-based resilience mechanism. Under stress, synchronized systems waste less of their remaining absorptive capacity on preventable divergence.

This mechanism defines alignment under stress as maintenance of sequence, scale, and variability compatibility when conditions become unstable. A stressed system still faces load and support challenges, but if those forces remain coordinated, the burden on liquidity and runway is reduced. Misaligned stressed systems experience the opposite outcome: stress is amplified because demand and support collide more often and more severely. Alignment therefore determines whether disruption is absorbed efficiently or inefficiently.

Across time, resilient systems preserve more function under stress because coordination remains sufficiently intact to prevent frequent avoidable pressure events. Fragile systems lose alignment as stress rises, which causes reserve use to increase and tolerance to fall faster. The same amount of adversity therefore produces different outcomes depending on whether synchronization survives disruption. Alignment acts as a force multiplier for all other stabilizing mechanisms.

The contrast shows that stress is not only about resource depth or demand size. It is also about whether the system remains coordinated while stressed. Role of alignment under stress therefore defines how synchronization supports resilience during disruption.

Stress containment versus stress amplification is the structural contrast between systems that absorb accumulated pressure and systems that convert that pressure into broader instability. Containment means that stress remains bounded within the system's absorptive and adaptive mechanisms. Amplification means that stress weakens those mechanisms and thereby increases future stress. This contrast defines whether disruption stabilizes into survivable stress or escalates into accelerating breakdown.

This mechanism defines containment as the successful absorption and distribution of stress, and amplification as the self-worsening response of a system under stress. In a contained system, liquidity, runway, flexibility, alignment, and constraint continue functioning well enough to prevent threshold breach. In an amplifying system, those same components weaken under pressure, causing new stress to arrive against a less capable structure. This creates compounding fragility rather than bounded stress.

Across time, resilient systems exhibit containment because stress is absorbed without materially increasing the system's future instability profile. Fragile systems exhibit amplification because each stress event leaves the system more exposed to the next. This changes the system from one experiencing stress to one being reshaped by stress. The long-run effect is faster threshold approach and lower disturbance tolerance.

The contrast shows that the decisive question under stress is not whether stress exists, but whether stress remains contained or becomes self-reinforcing. Stress containment versus stress amplification therefore defines the core divergence between resilient and unstable stress response.

Resilience as a function of prior design means that stability under stress is determined primarily by structural conditions built into the system before disruption occurs. A system does not become resilient at the moment of stress; it reveals the resilience or fragility already embedded in its architecture. This makes resilience the outcome of prior expense design rather than of reactive response alone. Under stress, structure is exposed rather than invented.

This mechanism defines prior design as the accumulated arrangement of baseline load, variability, liquidity, runway, flexibility, alignment, and constraint before stress becomes active. These features determine whether pressure is absorbed, whether reserve use remains tolerable, whether load can adjust, and whether thresholds stay distant enough to preserve function. Stress therefore acts as a test of architecture. The outcome is shaped by preexisting structure, not by post hoc improvisation.

Across time, resilient systems continue functioning under disruption because their earlier design choices created enough absorptive depth and adjustment capacity to contain stress. Fragile systems fail because they entered disruption with thin reserves, rigid load, weak coordination, or poor boundaries. These systems may appear stable under normal conditions, but stress reveals the absence of durable design. The divergence is therefore not accidental; it is architectural.

The contrast makes the chapter's central claim explicit. Stability under stress is not a reaction layer added after disruption begins. It is the consequence of structure that existed before disruption arrived. Resilience as a function of prior design therefore defines why system outcome under stress is determined by architecture, not by improvisation.

The Continuity of Controlled Outflow

Controlled outflow is defined as load applied within the structural limits of the system so that expenses remain absorbable as they move across time. It is not simply lower outflow, nor is it reactive suppression after instability has appeared. It is the condition in which demand is bounded, distributed, and coordinated before it becomes disruptive. This makes controlled outflow the operational form of expense behavior.

This mechanism integrates prior system components by treating control, constraint, reduction, and smoothing as interacting properties of how load is allowed to exist. Control limits open-ended demand, constraint defines boundaries, reduction lowers persistent burden, and smoothing stabilizes timing and distribution. None of these alone defines stable outflow, but together they determine whether expenses arrive in a form the system can continuously absorb. Controlled outflow is therefore a structural state, not a single tactic or momentary condition.

Across time, controlled outflow preserves functional continuity because each interval of demand remains inside the system's absorptive range. Stable systems do not depend on perfect conditions for expenses to remain manageable; their outflow is already shaped to remain compatible with capacity under ordinary fluctuation. Unstable systems, by contrast, apply load in ways that exceed structural limits, forcing pressure, reserve use, and eventual stress.

The contrast shows that outflow becomes stable not when it disappears, but when it is consistently governable. Controlled outflow therefore defines the expense side of system stability as bounded demand maintained within structural limits.

Continuity is defined as sustained system operation across time without repeated breakdown in the relationship between load and capacity. It is not a single period of balance, but the persistence of absorbable outflow through changing intervals. This makes continuity the temporal condition of stability rather than its momentary appearance. A system is stable only if it can remain stable over time.

This mechanism integrates earlier concepts by showing that continuity depends on the prevention of recurring sequencing gaps, unmanaged variability, reserve exhaustion, and stress accumulation. Baseline must remain supportable, liquidity must remain operative, runway must remain sufficient, and load must remain coordinated with inflow. Continuity therefore is not produced by any one feature, but by the sustained cooperation of all stabilizing mechanisms. It is the time-expression of system coherence.

Across time, continuous systems absorb change without converting every disturbance into instability. They may experience pressure, but that pressure does not regularly break function or force structural deterioration. Discontinuous systems experience recurring interruptions in absorbability, causing reserves to thin, mismatch to intensify, and stress to accumulate. The system loses continuity when ordinary operation repeatedly crosses into instability.

The contrast shows that continuity is more demanding than temporary balance. A system can appear stable in one interval while being structurally discontinuous across many intervals. Continuity therefore defines the sustained operating state in which stable expense behavior persists over time.

System integration occurs when previously distinct mechanisms function together as one operating structure rather than as isolated conditions. This is the point at which baseline, variability, liquidity, runway, alignment, flexibility, and constraint stop appearing as separate topics and become interdependent parts of a single system. The expense structure is stable only when these mechanisms operate in coordination. A system is not the sum of definitions, but the interaction of active components.

This mechanism defines integration as the transition from analytic distinction to operating unity. Baseline defines the structural floor, margin measures distance from failure, smoothing reduces concentration, alignment synchronizes inflow and outflow, liquidity absorbs short-term mismatch, runway expresses duration, flexibility enables adaptation, and resilience determines stress tolerance. Each mechanism solves only part of the stability problem in isolation. System behavior emerges from how they combine.

Across time, integrated systems preserve coherence because each mechanism reinforces the others rather than compensating for their absence indefinitely. A system with liquidity but without alignment may survive, but at increasing reserve cost. A system with low baseline but without flexibility may remain stable under calm conditions and then fail under change. Integration matters because stability depends on coordinated function across layers, not strength in one layer alone.

The contrast shows that isolated strengths do not equal systemic stability. Stable systems integrate mechanisms into one structure, while unstable systems rely on fragments that cannot fully support each other. From mechanisms to system therefore defines the transition from component analysis to whole-system operation.

Load distribution is the core driver of expense stability because how demand is applied across time determines whether the system experiences continuity or repeated pressure. Magnitude matters, but distribution governs whether magnitude arrives in absorbable form. This gives temporal pattern a central role in system behavior. Outflow that is structurally supportable in total can still become destabilizing through poor distribution.

This mechanism integrates variability, clustering, smoothing, and timing by treating distribution as the common structure beneath them. Variability describes fluctuation, clustering concentrates load, smoothing redistributes it, and timing governs when it meets support. Together they define whether demand arrives as continuous flow or destabilizing spikes. Distribution therefore is not one feature among many, but the pattern logic through which load becomes stable or unstable.

Across time, systems with stable distribution preserve absorbability because load arrives in repeatable, bounded intervals that capacity can support. Systems with unstable distribution repeatedly convert ordinary demand into sequencing gaps, spikes, and reserve drawdown. This gradually weakens liquidity, shortens runway, and increases stress even without large changes in total expenses. Distribution therefore shapes not only immediate pressure but long-run system condition.

The contrast shows that instability often begins with how load is arranged rather than with how much load exists. Systems with well-formed distribution remain stable under conditions that concentrated systems cannot tolerate. Load distribution as the core driver therefore defines why pattern, not total alone, governs expense stability.

Alignment is system synchronization between inflow and outflow across timing, magnitude, and variability. It is the condition in which support and demand are coordinated so that load arrives in forms that the income structure can absorb with minimal friction. This makes alignment a central integrating mechanism rather than a secondary refinement. Stability requires not only support and demand, but a synchronized relationship between them.

This mechanism integrates timing alignment, magnitude fit, and variability coordination into one structural logic of compatibility. Outflow can remain controlled and still become destabilizing if it is badly timed relative to inflow. Inflow can be sufficient in aggregate and still fail if its structure does not match the load it must support. Alignment resolves this by making the operating patterns of both sides structurally compatible. It is therefore the synchronization layer of the system.

Across time, aligned systems reduce avoidable reserve use because ordinary demand is more often met directly by appropriately structured support. Misaligned systems rely on liquidity not only for shock or disruption, but to compensate for preventable divergence between inflow and outflow. This accelerates depletion and weakens continuity. Alignment therefore reduces both immediate mismatch and long-term instability.

The contrast shows that stable operation depends on coordinated structure, not only on adequate totals. Systems with alignment preserve continuity more efficiently, while systems without it pay a constant penalty in friction and reserve use. Alignment as system synchronization therefore defines how load and support operate together as one structure.

Smoothing is the stabilization of load patterns through temporal redistribution, and predictability is the emergent operating condition that follows from that stabilization. When demand is not clustered into destabilizing intervals, the system can anticipate how outflow will behave and preserve more reliable alignment with capacity. This makes smoothing a system-level contributor to continuity, not merely a local adjustment to pattern. Predictability is what stable distribution produces across time.

This mechanism integrates smoothing with variability, timing, liquidity, and alignment. By reducing spikes and irregular clustering, smoothing lowers pressure frequency, reduces unnecessary liquidity draw, and makes inflow-outflow coordination easier to sustain. Predictability is not imposed externally; it arises when distribution remains repeatable enough to support stable absorption. Smoothing therefore acts as a structural precondition for reliable operation under ordinary conditions.

Across time, smoothed systems maintain more stable reserve behavior and less erratic runway degradation because load arrives in bounded, repeatable forms. Unsmoothed systems repeatedly force the system into reactive absorption because each concentrated interval behaves like a partial shock. Predictability declines, reserve use rises, and stress becomes harder to contain. The result is a system whose instability is generated by pattern disorder rather than by sheer scale alone.

The contrast shows that smoothing changes the character of outflow by changing its temporal form. Systems with stable pattern become more predictable and therefore more stable, while systems without pattern stability remain exposed to recurring disruption. Smoothing and predictability therefore define how distributional order supports continuity.

Constraint is the boundary layer that limits load before it forms, and control is the broader structural organization that keeps outflow inside absorptive limits once those boundaries are active. Together they prevent the expense system from becoming open-ended, self-amplifying, or dependent on repeated reactive correction. This makes them core components of controlled outflow. Stability requires both defined limits and an operating structure that respects them.

This mechanism integrates pre-load regulation with bounded magnitude, pathway control, and non-escalating system behavior. Constraint determines what load is allowed to become; control determines how allowed load behaves within the system. Without constraint, demand can expand beyond sustainable bounds. Without control, even bounded load can become destabilizing through poor distribution, weak coordination, or reserve-intensive operation. The two therefore function as complementary stabilizers.

Across time, constrained and controlled systems preserve continuity because load remains inside known ranges and enters through stable pathways. Systems lacking these properties are more vulnerable to drift, feedback escalation, spike concentration, and instability under change. They spend more of their operation compensating for preventable demand structure rather than absorbing unavoidable demand. This weakens every other stabilizing layer.

The contrast shows that stability does not emerge from reactive containment alone. Systems with embedded limits and structured load behavior remain absorbable longer and more consistently than systems that merely respond after overload appears. Constraint and control therefore define the preventive architecture of stable outflow.

Baseline is the persistent minimum load that must be sustained for system operation, and structural limits are the conditions that determine whether that baseline remains supportable without compressing the entire system. Together they define the lower boundary of stable outflow. No stability model is complete without identifying what demand cannot disappear and how far that demand sits from failure. This makes baseline the foundational limit condition of the system.

This mechanism integrates the expense floor, margin, drift, and boundary conditions by treating baseline as the structural floor over which all other demand layers operate. If baseline is too high relative to capacity, every additional stressor becomes more destabilizing because the system begins from compression rather than from usable distance. Structural limits matter because they determine whether baseline remains inside the supportable range. Stability begins not with optional load, but with what must continuously be carried.

Across time, systems with supportable baseline and preserved margin absorb variability, timing shifts, and moderate disruption more effectively. Systems whose baseline approaches capacity operate in a narrow band where ordinary fluctuation quickly becomes pressure. Drift further weakens them by raising the floor over time, reducing the space available for absorption. Baseline therefore is not merely the starting point of demand; it is the structural condition that shapes all later resilience.

The contrast shows that stable outflow cannot be understood only through variable patterns or reserve depth. The system's minimum operating requirement determines how much room exists for everything else. Baseline and structural limits therefore define the foundational boundary of continuity.

Liquidity is the stabilizing buffer that provides immediate absorptive capacity when load and inflow do not align perfectly in real time. It does not create stable structure by itself, but it allows a stable structure to survive unavoidable sequence gaps, modest shocks, and bounded fluctuation without immediate failure. This makes liquidity the short-term operational layer of continuity. Where alignment, smoothing, and control reduce mismatch, liquidity absorbs the mismatch that remains.

This mechanism integrates reserve function with pressure containment, timing mismatch bridging, and stress prevention. Liquidity allows continuity to persist when support and demand are temporarily out of phase. Without it, even small divergence between load and capacity turns into direct pressure. With it, the system gains a practical means of converting temporary mismatch into manageable drawdown rather than immediate instability. Liquidity therefore is the system's present-tense stabilizer.

Across time, stable systems preserve liquidity because their outflow is structured well enough that reserves are not consumed to compensate for constant preventable disorder. Unstable systems depend on liquidity as a substitute for alignment, smoothing, or flexibility, which accelerates depletion and weakens future absorption. The same buffer becomes either a stabilizer or a decaying compensation layer depending on overall design. This is why liquidity cannot be separated from the system that uses it.

The contrast shows that reserves matter most when structure is already sound enough to let them buffer rather than permanently compensate. Liquidity as stabilizing buffer therefore defines the immediate absorptive layer of controlled continuity.

Runway is the time dimension of system viability, expressing how long liquidity can sustain outflow under current conditions. If liquidity is the stock of short-term capacity, runway is the duration that stock can continue supporting load before failure threshold is reached. This makes runway the temporal extension of the system's reserve condition. Stability is therefore not only a question of what the system can absorb now, but how long it can continue absorbing over time.

This mechanism integrates load rate, depletion speed, pressure, and reserve duration into a single temporal model. A system with the same liquidity can have radically different runway depending on how outflow is structured. Controlled outflow preserves runway because reserves are consumed more slowly and less erratically. Uncontrolled outflow compresses runway by raising reserve dependence and increasing the rate of depletion. Runway therefore reflects the cumulative effect of all other system properties on time-to-failure.

Across time, stable systems exhibit more consistent runway because depletion occurs under bounded, aligned, and adaptable demand conditions. Unstable systems experience unstable runway behavior because reserve use is driven by spikes, misalignment, rigid load, or stress amplification. This means that time itself becomes a diagnostic of system coherence. Runway is not just remaining duration; it is the temporal expression of structural quality.

The contrast shows that continuity requires more than immediate absorbability. It requires enough time capacity to absorb ongoing stress without rapid collapse. Runway as time dimension therefore defines the duration layer of stable operation.

Flexibility is the adjustability of load, and adaptability is the system's capacity to use that adjustability to remain stable under changing conditions. Together they determine whether continuity can survive change or only calm conditions. This makes flexibility and adaptability essential integrative mechanisms in the final operating model. A stable system must not only be absorbable in one state; it must be reconfigurable across states.

This mechanism integrates rigid versus flexible load, response to inflow disruption, and stress tolerance under variability or shock. Flexibility allows adjustments in timing, magnitude, or presence of load. Adaptability organizes those adjustments into a coherent response that preserves continuity when conditions shift. Without these properties, every change in inflow, reserve level, or variability must be absorbed without load-side movement. That makes the system brittle.

Across time, adaptable systems preserve stability because they can reduce mismatch before it hardens into repeated reserve depletion or failure. Non-adaptable systems may remain stable temporarily, but they do so only while conditions stay narrow enough to support fixed demand. Once those conditions move, instability accelerates because the system lacks an internal method of reconfiguration. Adaptability therefore distinguishes durable stability from conditional stability.

The contrast shows that long-term continuity requires more than strong reserves or low baseline. It requires a load structure capable of changing with conditions. Flexibility and adaptability therefore define the system's capacity to remain stable through movement rather than only through stasis.

Stress containment is the prevention of accumulated pressure from escalating into broader system instability. It is the point at which the system's stabilizing mechanisms continue to absorb stress rather than amplifying it. This makes containment the resilience function of controlled outflow. A stable system is not one that never encounters stress, but one in which stress does not spread into uncontrolled deterioration.

This mechanism integrates pressure, stress, liquidity, runway, flexibility, and alignment into a single resilience process. Pressure becomes stress when imbalance repeats or remains unresolved; stress becomes destabilizing when the system's absorptive and adaptive mechanisms begin to fail. Containment interrupts that progression. It keeps stress bounded within recoverable ranges by preserving reserve function, load adjustability, coordinated support, and non-amplifying load structure.

Across time, systems with strong containment remain functional under disruption because each stress event does not materially increase the probability of subsequent breakdown. Systems without containment do the opposite: stress weakens the structure, making future stress more damaging. This creates amplification rather than resilience. The system then becomes progressively more fragile even if the original pressure event was moderate.

The contrast shows that the decisive issue is not whether stress exists, but whether stress remains bounded. Systems that contain stress preserve continuity; systems that amplify stress move toward failure. Stress containment therefore defines the resilience layer of the final stability model.

Failure conditions occur when controlled, aligned, and absorbable outflow can no longer be maintained across time. This happens when reserve absorption fails, runway becomes insufficient, structural limits are breached, or coordination between system mechanisms collapses. Failure therefore is not one event but a condition in which continuity has broken. It marks the loss of viable system operation under existing structure.

This mechanism integrates breakdown across baseline compression, reserve exhaustion, misalignment, rigid load, uncontrolled variability, and stress amplification. A system fails when its mechanisms no longer function together as one coordinated structure. Liquidity is no longer enough to buffer, runway is too short to sustain stress, flexibility cannot reduce mismatch sufficiently, and alignment has weakened enough that ordinary load repeatedly becomes unabsorbable. Failure is therefore the endpoint of de-coordination.

Across time, stable systems remain distant from these conditions because their architecture preserves multiple layers of containment. Unstable systems move closer as drift raises baseline, reserves erode, pressure repeats, and mechanisms increasingly compensate for each other's weaknesses rather than reinforcing one another. This creates a narrowing path of viability. Once continuity breaks, the system no longer operates in a stable state even if some resources remain.

The contrast shows that failure is not defined solely by zero resources or one dramatic event. It is defined by the collapse of coordinated system function. Failure conditions therefore mark the point where continuity of controlled outflow no longer exists.

Stable versus unstable systems is the full-system contrast between expense structures whose mechanisms coordinate into continuity and expense structures whose mechanisms repeatedly diverge into pressure, depletion, and stress. This contrast is not based on one variable alone. It is based on whether the entire operating model functions as an integrated structure across time. Stability is therefore systemic coherence, while instability is systemic fragmentation.

This mechanism integrates every major layer of the model. Stable systems maintain supportable baseline, bounded variability, smoothed distribution, coordinated alignment, preserved liquidity, durable runway, adaptable load, effective constraint, and contained stress. Unstable systems exhibit the opposite pattern: compressed floor-to-capacity distance, concentration of load, sequencing failure, reserve-intensive operation, rigid demand, and amplification of stress. The difference is not merely descriptive. It is operational.

Across time, stable systems preserve continuity because each mechanism reduces burden on the others. Unstable systems degrade because each weakness increases pressure on the remaining stabilizers until they also begin to fail. This means that unstable systems are not simply "weaker" versions of stable systems. They are systems whose mechanisms do not cooperate. Stability is therefore a pattern of coordination, while instability is a pattern of escalating mismatch.

The contrast shows that the final distinction is architectural, not motivational or episodic. Stable versus unstable systems therefore defines the whole-system difference between coordinated continuity and cumulative structural failure.

The continuous operating state is the final definition of system stability: load remains continuously controlled, aligned, and absorbable across time. It is the condition in which outflow does not merely stay within occasional limits, but functions within a durable operating structure that preserves continuity under ordinary variation and bounded disruption. This makes stability an ongoing system condition rather than a temporary result. The expense system is stable when its operation remains viable over time.

This mechanism integrates the full model into one unified operating definition. Controlled outflow keeps demand within structural limits. Baseline remains supportable, smoothing stabilizes pattern, alignment synchronizes support and load, constraint prevents overload, liquidity buffers residual mismatch, runway preserves temporal viability, flexibility enables adaptation, and resilience contains stress. Stability exists when these mechanisms coordinate into one continuous mode of operation rather than functioning as isolated protections.

Across time, the continuous operating state preserves viability because no single disturbance is forced to carry the whole system. Demand remains organized enough that capacity can absorb it, and support remains coordinated enough that reserves are not permanently consumed by preventable mismatch. Unstable systems lose this operating state when outflow becomes irregular, misaligned, reserve-intensive, or structurally uncontained. Continuity then breaks, and system stability dissolves into episodic compensation and eventual failure.

The contrast makes the final definition explicit. Stability is not low spending, temporary balance, or isolated reserve depth. Stability is continuous, controlled, and aligned outflow across time. The continuous operating state therefore defines the unified model of expense stability.

About the Author

Mark Ellison writes about structural durability in systems exposed to volatility.

His work focuses on long-horizon stability across financial architecture, career positioning, cognitive resilience, and physical capacity. Rather than treating these domains as separate disciplines, he approaches them as interdependent systems governed by load, margin, buffer depth, and threshold behavior.

The Stability framework examines how fragility accumulates gradually and how disciplined structural calibration preserves optionality across decades. The objective is not optimization for peak outcomes, but preservation of functional continuity under variance.

Money Stability is part of a broader multi-domain stability ecosystem developed under Perennial Publishing, each domain addressing a distinct vector of long-term durability.

The work is designed for readers who prefer structural clarity over motivational rhetoric and long-horizon coherence over short-term intensity.

The Money Stability Series

Money Stability*: How to Build Financial Control in an Unstable World* (Cornerstone Volume)

Liquidity and Runway: *How to Build Financial Time, Extend Your Runway, and Stay Stable in an Unstable Economy*

Income Stability: *How to Build Predictable, Durable, and Resilient Income*

Expense Stability: *How to Control Spending, Reduce Leakage, and Create Consistency*

Future titles expand the Money Stability framework:

Cash Flow Stability
Reserve Stability
Income Durability

Part of a Broader Stability Framework

The Money Stability Series is part of a larger stability ecosystem published by Perennial Publishing.

Related domains include:

Metabolic Stability — biological load, energy, and recovery capacity

Career Stability — income durability, positioning, and transition resilience

Mental Stability — cognitive steadiness under pressure and uncertainty

Emotional Stability — regulatory steadiness in environments that do not slow down

Each domain approaches stability as a structural problem: capacity versus load, buffers versus shocks, and governance versus drift. Together, they form a unified framework for long-horizon durability across the major systems that determine life trajectory.

About Perennial Publishing

Perennial Publishing produces practical systems guides for building stability in an unstable world.

Our books explore the foundations of long-term resilience across health, finance, career, and everyday decision-making. Each title focuses on clear frameworks, durable principles, and practical strategies that help readers build lasting stability rather than short-term fixes.

The Perennial catalog includes series on metabolic health, financial stability, career systems, and personal consistency. While each book stands on its own, they share a common goal: helping individuals create durable systems that support a stable and sustainable life.

For bulk or institutional orders, contact Perennial Publishing.

Made in the USA
Monee, IL
05 November 2026

68005264R00142